Isobel Kuhn

Lights in Lisuland

Isobel Kuhn

Lights in Lisuland

by Irene Howat

Christian Focus Publications

© Copyright 2001
Christian Focus Publications

ISBN: 1-85792-610-2

Published 2001, reprinted 2004
by
Christian Focus Publications Ltd.
Geanies House, Fearn, Ross-shire,
IV20 1TW, Scotland, Great Britain.

www.christianfocus.com
email: info@christianfocus.com

Cover design by Owen Daily
Illustrated by Norma Burgin

Printed and bound by Cox and Wyman

DEDICATION
for
Kenneth and Isabel,
Harry and June

INTRODUCTION

The story of Isobel Kuhn inspired me as a teenager, and it has inspired me anew as I researched it in order to write this book. It's a very human story. Isobel, who was for 26 years a missionary, first in China thcn in Thailand, was a woman of great passion. She was passionately in love with her husband John, yet had to leave him free to travel for long periods of time in the course of his work. Isobel was passionately in love with Kathryn and Danny, her son and daughter, but had to endure years of separation from them, sometimes in the most trying of circumstances. Her love for the people of Lisuland was passionate, and the account of her service there is inspiring.

Isobel Kuhn, who had a passion for life, died in her fifties. What a lot she packed into those years.

Irene Howat

Contents

Contents

Mrs. Twenty Questions

At noon, on the 11th October 1928, *The Empress of Russia* edged away from Vancouver Wharf. Bugle notes poured their farewells into the air from the bridge of the ship. And dozens of young women waved from the shore to another young woman, who stood on the deck waving back. Suddenly the group on shore burst into song which was only drowned out by the creak of the anchors rising. Paper streamers filled the air, falling down slowly in the noontide heat onto the tearful faces of those standing watching as the *Empress* left port and left Canada.

'Who do you think she is?' Charlotte Jackson asked her husband. 'She must be famous with a send-off like that.'

'How would I know that?' he replied, in an American drawl. 'But I'm sure you'll nosey it out.'

Mrs. Jackson winced. 'I'm not nosey!' she announced. 'I'm just interested in people.'

'Same difference,' he winked, and she ignored him.

Within forty-eight hours Charlotte Jackson had cornered her prey and discovered where she was going and why.

'What makes a girl like you want to go to China as a missionary?' she probed.

Isobel Miller looked far into the distance. She thought about all the reasons for going to China. She thought about her new husband, the new name she would have soon, Isobel Kuhn. But she wasn't going out to China just to marry John Kuhn. There were other reasons, more important ones. The sea was calm and there was no land to be seen in any direction. Most of the other passengers were taking a siesta in their cabins.

Turning to her companion of the last half-hour, Isobel answered, 'I'm going to China, not just because I want to, but because I believe God wants me to.'

The woman's smile didn't quite hide her detective intentions. 'Well I sure hope you know what you're doing,' she said in her Southern American accent. 'But if you were my daughter I'd be mighty sorry to see you leave for a life of dirt and disease in some Chinese village that's too small even to be in an atlas.'

Seeing the discomfort in Isobel's eyes, she continued. 'Isn't that what your mother says?'

Feeling that this was too personal a question to answer without even knowing the questioner's name, Isobel took refuge in finding that out.

'My name is Mrs. Jackson, Mrs. Charlotte Jackson,' was the reply. 'My husband and I are going round the world. We started off from Swannee in Texas three weeks ago. Mr. Jackson is something of an adventurer. But while he's having his adventures I'll be tucked up somewhere safe and comfortable.'

Isobel nodded, grateful to leave the subject of her mother behind.

'And that's just what a young lady like you should be, safe and comfortable, not missioning in the Chinese outback. I'm quite sure your poor dear mother would agree with me.'

'My mother is dead,' said the girl softly.

She was taken by the arm and led to a row of deckchairs. Mrs. Jackson's nosiness made her like a terrier sniffing out a rat.

'Sit down,' she demanded, 'and tell me all about it.'

Isobel swallowed hard. Well, she thought to herself, I've got a choice. I can tell her why I feel called to be a missionary in China or I can answer awkward questions about the family - and I'm not doing that.

Taking her companion's hesitation as sorrow, Mrs. Jackson took Isobel by the hand. 'Just treat me as an aunt, dear, and pour it all out.'

When she said that, Isobel may have looked serious but inwardly she was smiling. You've asked for it, she thought, now you'll get it … now listen to the testimony of Isobel Miller.

'I was brought up in a Christian home and just accepted all that my parents taught me,' the girl began.

Mrs. Jackson nodded approvingly.

'But when I was at university one of my lecturers challenged that, saying that people who believed that God was the Creator, only did so because their parents had told them that. I thought about that and decided that he was quite right. I stopped going to church, stopped reading my Bible and started doing all sorts of things I'd never done before.'

Isobel, noting Mrs. Jackson's raised eyebrows, went on with her story. 'I fell in love with another student and we became secretly engaged ... but he two-timed me. When I found that out I was devastated. It was as though my whole world had fallen apart. I couldn't study, I couldn't enjoy anything and I couldn't sleep. One night, when I thought that everyone else in the house had been asleep for hours, Dad came into my bedroom, knelt by my bed and prayed for me. "Your prayers don't go further than the ceiling," I told him. How that must have hurt him.'

Her companion opened her mouth to speak, but Isobel didn't notice. She was reliving the events of that terrible time.

'Just before Christmas that year I'd had enough. I decided to commit suicide. There was a bottle of poison in the bathroom, and one night I got out of bed and fully intended to drink it all. As I grasped the bathroom door, I heard three long groans from my parents' room. Dad was moaning in his sleep. My mind raced. If I kill myself, Dad will think I've gone to hell. There's no such place as hell, but that's what he would think. Could I make Dad that unhappy? Though I longed to die, I couldn't put that curse on my father. I staggered back to my bedroom. "God," I whispered, "if there is a God, if you will prove to me that you exist, and if you will give me peace, I will give you my whole life. I'll do anything you ask me to do, go where you send me, obey you all my days." And I laid my aching head on my pillow and pulled the blankets up to shut out the world.'

'My poor child,' gasped Mrs. Jackson, dramatically wiping a non-existent tear from the corner of her eye. 'I have two daughters myself and it would break my heart if I thought they suffered so.'

'But the wonderful thing,' continued Isobel, 'was that I slept! The first I knew it was morning. Now, that made me think. Was it just a fluke, or had God really answered my prayer and given me peace? And if he had, where did that leave me? I'd promised to serve him if he answered my prayer. What was I to do now? I decided to search for God through what was written about Jesus Christ in the Gospels.'

Her American companion's eyebrows arched.

'As far as my parents were concerned I was just the same rebellious daughter, not going to church and not reading my Bible. But one day Mum invited me to a meeting. I went with her and was glad I did. The speaker wasn't just preaching about Jesus, a man he had read all about. I knew from how he spoke that he was speaking about Jesus, his personal friend.'

'I'm not sure we can go quite that far,' objected Mrs. Jackson. 'That seems a little presumptuous. But go on with your story. I'm enjoying it.'

Isobel smiled. 'By then I was a primary school teacher and living in lodgings as my parents had moved away from Vancouver.'

'You must have loved that,' the older woman said. 'Primary children are such cute little things. Why, I think I'd have enjoyed doing that myself!'

'Cute they might be, but enjoyable they were not,'

commented Isobel sadly. 'They ran rings round me! I felt I was such a poor teacher that I signed up for an extra teaching course in the school holiday. It was held in Seattle and I stayed with Mrs. Whipple, a friend of my father.

Mrs. Jackson stifled a giggle. 'What an amusing name,' she said.

This is turning into quite a long story, Isobel thought, but my companion doesn't seem to be tiring. I suppose she has nothing better to do for hours on end at sea.

'Mrs. Whipple is one of the most comfortable people I know,' Isobel went on. 'She didn't force her beliefs on me and only spoke about Christianity when I brought up the subject. Before I left, she invited me to The Firs Bible Conference which was to be held in the summer. However, I had already arranged to go on another teaching course, and said I'd be unable to attend. But in the end I was able to go, and my time there changed my world.'

'I hope you're not going to preach at me,' cautioned the older lady. 'That would not be ladylike.'

Isobel shook her head.

'Mrs. Whipple didn't do that to me, and I won't do it to you.'

Mrs. Jackson laughed. 'Well, I won't get a better deal in town than that!'

'At The Firs, it was in the summer of 1923, I shared a room with a woman called Edna. Edna and her husband were missionaries in China. When they were on holiday, he dived into a mountain pool to save a young man who had cramp. He did save his friend's life, but it cost him his own. She made such an impression on me. Despite all her sadness she still knew the joy of the Lord. It was she who challenged me to go overseas to serve the Lord. And what could I say? Had I not promised to serve him when and where he wanted if he would answer my prayer?'

'But aren't there enough people in Canada who need to hear the Bible message, without you going to the other side of the world, and to places that don't even have proper toilets?' said Mrs Jackson, shuddering at the thought.

'I had promised to go where the Lord wanted me,' Isobel said, a little more firmly.

'And how did you know he wanted you in China?'

'I'm coming to that,' Isobel assured her companion, 'but our chairs are now in the shade. Shall we move to a sunnier spot?'

The two women walked round the deck in silence for some time before deciding on the warmest and most comfortable deckchairs and settling down on them.

'Do go on,' instructed Mrs. Jackson, whose nosiness had overtaken her politeness.

'I taught for another year and went back to The Firs the following summer. Mr J. O. Fraser of the China Inland Mission was one of the speakers. I'd never heard of him before I went, but I'll not forget him for as long as I live. He told us how the Lord had led him there, and he described the work he did. As he spoke, my heart ached to be in China, to be with the people he was telling us about, to tell the demon worshippers about Jesus, to teach the illiterate people how to read the Bible, to hold the children on my knee and tell them that Jesus loved little children. At the end of his talk, Mr. Fraser appealed for men to answer God's call to go with the Gospel to China. Everything in me ached to go, but I wasn't a man. Would a young woman be any good? Could God use me in China?'

'And can he, I wonder?' said Mrs. Jackson, quite sure that the answer was no.

Isobel ignored that comment, after all, she had still to find that out for herself. And Mrs. Jackson made no objection when she went on with her story.

'In order to prepare for the mission field, I applied to Bible School. The one I went to was decided by a lady I'd met at The Firs, a dear and generous lady who paid my fare to the Moody Bible Institute in Chicago and funded my first year's college and boarding fees!'

'You studied in Chicago! You went to America! Perhaps you're not the backwoods girl I took you for after all,' announced Mrs. Jackson, more than a little unkindly.

Isobel smiled at her directness. 'I'm being direct too,' she reminded herself.

'Yes,' she said, 'I studied in America and I visited Chicago's slums and prisons and hospitals with the good news that Jesus saves.'

'I hope you saw some of the beautiful places too,' the older lady said, sounding rather miffed, 'America is not all slums and prisons.'

'There wasn't time or money for sightseeing,' Isobel admitted, 'however, I did see a lot of lovely and exciting things. But,' she smiled shyly, 'the loveliest and most exciting thing of all was meeting a very special young man. His name is John Kuhn.'

Mrs. Jackson put her hand over her mouth to hide a yawn. 'This sounds like a happy ending,' she said, 'but may we keep it until tomorrow after lunch? I told my husband I wouldn't have a siesta and now I can't keep my eyes open.'

She rose. 'Until tomorrow.'

'Until tomorrow.'

Isobel smiled broadly. But her thoughts were not of Mrs. Charlotte Jackson, they were of John Kuhn.Isobel smiled as she remembered her first sight of John, busy in the Bible College kitchen. Memories flooded back, of the instant attraction she had felt for him, of the months she had avoided John as she believed that she should remain single, and of God's goodness in bringing them together, allowing them to fall in love and calling them both to service in China. Isobel sighed. 'One day I'll tell our children about that', she thought, it's so romantic.

While Mrs. Jackson had nothing to do with herself on board the ship, Isobel did. For an hour each day an experienced missionary, Ruth Paxton, gave the mission's new recruits an hour of Bible teaching. When Isobel emerged from the cabin and went on deck the first person she saw was Charlotte Jackson.

'I've kept a deckchair for you,' the older woman said. 'And I can't wait to hear the rest of your story. But I've two questions I'd like to ask you first?'

Isobel waited for the questions. She wondered what the lady would want to know more about. But her queries were about something else entirely.

'I couldn't help but notice that you meet with all your friends for a while each day. I just wondered what you did behind that closed cabin door.'

The girl smiled to herself. Was there no end of this woman's cheek? she wondered.

'We meet for Bible teaching,' she explained. 'I'm learning such a lot there.'

Mrs. Jackson shook her head sadly. 'I've got to say this to you as you're a poor motherless girl ...'

Isobel wondered what on earth was coming next!

'... but too much religion is not good for anyone, far less a pretty little girl. You'll never find a husband if all you go to is Bible classes.'

The woman's face was a picture when Isobel told her that she was engaged to John Kuhn, and that he also went to Bible classes, and that he was already a missionary in China!

'I think you had another question?' Isobel said.

For once Mrs. Jackson looked just a little uncomfortable. But her inquisitiveness swallowed her pride. 'I couldn't help but notice the long line of young women who were there to wave you off at Vancouver.'

Isobel turned to look out to sea, not because there was anything there to look at, but to avoid her companion seeing her grinning face. Now she knew why the grand lady was so interested in her!

Arranging her face in a suitable expression, Isobel faced Mrs. Jackson and explained.

'Yesterday,' she began, 'I told you that I studied at

Moody Bible Institute in Chicago. When I graduated from there last year, I went to live with my father and brother in Vancouver. My mother died while I was a student. Although China Inland Mission provisionally accepted me, I could not go right out. Among other reasons there was an anti-foreign uprising at the time. For over a year I worked as superintendent to the Vancouver Girls' Corner Club. The young ladies you saw at the wharf were members of the Club.'

'Well, well,' said Mrs. Jackson. 'So that's who they were!'

Having satisfied her curiosity, she rose from the deckchair. 'I've so enjoyed getting to know you,' she told Isobel. 'Now I must go and find Mr. Jackson. He'll be rising from his siesta I'm sure.'

The young missionary watched the lady go. What a disappointment that was to her, she said to herself. She thought she'd met a celebrity!

Isobel walked over to the rail and leant on it. 'I must be facing east,' she decided from the direction of the sun, 'east towards China, towards John and towards the Lisu people.'

In at the Deep End

'Well, Mrs. Kuhn,' John said to his wife of just a few weeks, as they walked to a poor village to visit the people there, 'may I ask what you think of marriage?'

Isobel grinned. 'I think now that we're man and wife, you could call me Isobel.'

John put on a look of mock horror. 'I wouldn't dream of such presumption!' he said. 'I think I'll just call you Sweetheart or Darling or something more formal like that. I fact, I think I rather like Belle.'

They giggled like children as they walked, but then they grew serious and stopped to pray a short distance from the end of their journey.

Isobel watched her husband walk through the village. 'Why is it,' she wondered, 'that he doesn't seem to mind the mosquitoes, the dirt and the smells? Look at him, he is walking right through the worst of it, as though he doesn't notice at all.' The Chinese people watched the white couple as they walked. Suddenly Isobel realised how important it was not to show the disgust she felt. Dozens of eyes were fixed on them.

'This is where we are going,' John said, leading her to one of the poorest homes in the village. 'Look, the family is waiting for us.'

They were welcomed warmly and taken into the house. Although she had studied at language school, Isobel still had to concentrate hard when taking part in conversations. Visits like this were hard work.

'Hello,' she said to the little girl who was reaching out to touch her white skin.

Two large dark eyes opened wide and two little hands stroked her arm. Suddenly Isobel noticed a boil on the back of the girl's hand, a nasty pus-filled boil. Instinct made her want to draw her arm away, but she caught John's eye and knew what she had to do. Reaching out, she lifted the little girl on to her knee, allowing two dirty hands to explore her arms, then her neck, then her hair. Her stomach heaved as she took in her surroundings. The child's mother was preparing a meal for them, two mangy dogs sniffed around the food, several other children arrived, their insides having told them that dinner was ready, and everyone crushed together round a low table. Isobel could just imagine the fun that lice and fleas were having hopping from one to the other. Although she truly tried to love the people, she thought that nothing could be worse than the situation she was in. But she was wrong.

The hostess produced a pile of cooked pork fat surrounded by rice. There was no meat whatever, just hot white pork fat.

'Oh John,' she said weakly, relieved that nobody else understood English, 'do I have to eat this? I'll be sick if I do.'

He smiled at his wife, who looked as if she might be

sick whether she ate it or not! Then he chose one of the larger pieces and put it in front of her. Isobel could hardly believe her eyes!

Still smiling, John said softly, 'When her back is turned give it to the friend under the table.'

Isobel's puzzlement showed on her face, then a smile spread from ear to ear. Suddenly the fleas and lice didn't seem to matter, the smell and dirt were of secondary importance, all her thoughts were centred on choosing the right moment to drop her pork fat under the table where one of the dogs would enjoy it thoroughly.

'You asked me what I thought of married life,' the young woman said to her husband as they left the village.

John turned and looked at her.

'I approve of it,' she smiled. 'I approve of it thoroughly. To have a husband who can get rid of a pound of pork fat and leave me with a plate of rice is a distinct improvement on being single and being sick.'

Suddenly Isobel's face was serious.

'What are you thinking?' John asked.

A tear trickled down her face. 'I was quite sure God wanted me to come to China,' she said. 'And I want to love it here, and I want to love the people and to tell them about Jesus, but everything gets in the way.'

Her husband sat her down by the roadside. 'Tell me what you mean,' he encouraged.

Isobel's tears flowed freely. 'I don't think I'll ever get used to the dirt and the smell, the lice and fleas make me itch all the time, even when I know I don't have any. And the food - the food is disgusting! It all smells sour and mouldy, and it tastes it too.'

John put his arm round his wife.

'Is that all?' he asked gently.

Hiding her face in her hands, Isobel went on. 'And I hate, I just hate having no privacy. Everyone sees everything. It's like being an exhibit in a zoo. I can't even get washed in peace. And the toilet arrangements ... they are unspeakable!'

There was a long silence.

John took a deep breath. 'Imagine what heaven is like,' he said, looking up into the blue afternoon sky. 'Everything there is perfect, beautiful, clean, sparkling, radiant. There are no words wonderful enough to describe it, are there?'

Isobel nodded her head, but wondered what he was getting at.

'I don't suppose,' he went on, 'that anyone would ever want to leave such a splendid place to go to somewhere dirty and poor and wretched. But that's just what Jesus did. He left the magnificent glories of heaven to come down to earth as a baby, to be born in a miserable stable, to grow up in an ordinary working home, to minister to sick men and women, even touching lepers, reaching out to the mad and the demon-possessed. And that wasn't all,' John continued, 'he, who had never done, said or even thought anything wrong in all of his 33 years, was nailed to a cross and crucified to pay the price for our sins. That's what Jesus did for us, Isobel. Can we not love our Chinese brothers and sisters for him?'

Bowing her head, Isobel prayed through her tears. 'Precious Jesus, forgive me. Thank you for leaving heaven's glories to save my soul. And thank you that we are here in China. Please, please help me to love these people, and to love serving you here. And please, Lord, please stop me focusing on the nasty things, and.....,' there was a long pause, '.... help me to like pork fat. That really will be to your glory. Amen.'

'Amen,' John added. 'Amen.'

Rising from the verge of the road, they set off together in the direction of home.

'Try not to bottle things up inside yourself,' John advised. 'Problems just get worse and worse if you don't share them. That's part of what being married is about, sharing things together.'

'I suppose I'm just not used to doing that. But I will try,' said Isobel rather hesitantly.

'Is there anything else bothering you?' John asked, acutely aware of his wife's hesitation.

She heaved a long sigh. 'Yes. There is.'

'Then share it.' It was a minute or two before Isobel spoke again.

'All right,' she agreed. 'I will, because it really is confusing me. At The Firs in 1924, I truly believed the Lord was calling me to be a missionary to the Lisu people away up in the mountains. It's 1930 now, so that's six years ago, and where are we? We're working with Chinese people, not Lisu, and the great plains here could hardly be more different from Lisuland!'

Her husband listened intently.

'And you seem quite settled here,' she added lamely. 'I think that's what bothers me most. How can God have called us to work in separate parts of China?'

'I don't think he's done that, dear,' John said. 'I'm happy to work here now because that's where the Mission has put us. Where we'll be in the future is not mine to know. Perhaps we'll be in Lisuland one day.'

'I hope so,' wished Isobel. 'I really, truly hope so for my heart is full of love for the Lisu.'

'Listen,' John said. 'You believe that the Lord used Mr. Fraser to call you to work with the Lisu. Right?'

She nodded. 'And you know that Mr. Fraser loves the people of Lisuland. Right?'

Isobel agreed. 'Yet we know that the Mission has appointed him to work as Superintendent, and to live in Shanghai for the time being. Do you think he loves the Lisu any less because of that?'

His wife shook her head.

'And do you think he would have kept us here if he thought it was right for us to minister to the people he loves so much?'

'No,' she agreed. 'I don't think he would.'

'So should we not be like Mr. Fraser, and work where the Mission puts us. One day, perhaps, they will send us to the Lisu.'

About a year later, the Kuhns were still on the plains. And they had just finished telling a group of people about the Lord Jesus. Isobel was quite used to her new nickname of "Ma-ma". All the locals used it now - even the children.

'Ma-ma,' a little Chinese boy said, taking Isobel's hand and looking up at her with a smile. She bent down, picked the child up, and gave him a hug. 'We'll come back another day,' she told him as his face crumpled into tears.

'I want Ma-ma,' the child wept even more. 'I love Ma-ma.'

Isobel knelt down, pulled the little boy to herself, and whispered in his ear. 'I love you too. And I'll come back to see you soon.'

In English, which no one else could understand, John said softly, 'I think your prayers have been answered. God has given you love for the Chinese.'

Isobel looked from John to the little boy and back again. 'Yes,' she thought, 'that's true, yet my heart is still in Lisuland. But, if I'm right about what I'm thinking, we'll not be there for some time yet.'

'Are you sure?' John Kuhn gasped, when Isobel told him her news the following week. 'Are you quite sure?'

'As sure as I can be at this stage,' she laughed. 'And you'll make a lovely dad.' Her husband's face was a picture of surprise and delight.

'I can just see you with a baby,' he said. 'Look how good you were with the Chinese children.'

'Having one of our own will be a little different,' she laughed. 'I'll not be able to leave our baby crying and tell him that we'll be back another day!'

'Things will certainly be different,' he agreed.

'But not quite everything,' she thought to herself. 'We'll still be here. It's strange, I thought our children would be brought up speaking the language of the Lisu, but it seems that they'll be brought up here, and that their first words will be in Chinese.'

And that is just what happened. Little Kathryn Kuhn was born while her parents were missionaries in the southwest plains of China. That's where she said her first words, took her first steps, and made her very first friends.

When Kathryn was two years old, a letter arrived for her parents.

'Tell me a story,' the child pleaded, as John re-read the letter. 'Kathryn like a story.'

Her father smiled down at her. 'This is a story for Daddy and Mummy,' he explained. 'Look,' he pointed at the pages, 'there are no pictures in this story.'

John read Mr. Fraser's letter aloud. 'I want your prayers for a very puzzling problem. There are two Lisu churches in the Upper Salween Canyon which came into being through the pioneering work of four Lisu evangelists. It cost one of them his life. These two flourishing little churches are six days travel apart.' Isobel watched John's face as he read.

'At the moment only one missionary couple are working there. The husband is with one congregation and his wife with the other. But I cannot allow that to go on. The woman is very brave to stay alone in such an isolated place, but I can't be responsible for her being separated from her husband for much longer, yet I have no one else to send.'

John and Isobel looked at each other. They talked about it, prayed about it and Isobel dreamed about it, then agreed that John should write to Mr. Fraser. Isobel watched as the pen formed the words. 'We believe that the Lord is leading us to the Upper Salween.' And her heart sang.

It was decided that the Kuhns should go for a trip to Lisuland.

'Isobel can judge from this trip whether she can stand the life there,' Mr. Fraser wrote in his reply.

It was in March 1934 that the Kuhns exchanged the flat plains for the mountains. Isobel's dream came true, and she was not disappointed.

One afternoon, while Kathryn was having a nap, Isobel wrote to a friend. 'The poverty, squalor and insects are worse than the plains. But it is so much easier to bear. I'll tell you why. When we lived in the peasant village we were shut up in the drabness of it all, and we couldn't get away. I couldn't even find a quiet place to sit and think. As soon as we left the village we came to the rice fields, and I could hardly sit down in a paddy field! I always felt so conspicuous, like a pea on a flat plate. It is so different here. The villages are just as dirty, maybe even more so, but all I need to do is lift up my eyes to the mountains, to the magnificent Alpine panoramas all around me, to see the beauty of God's creation. And I can be private. Just ten minutes' walk out of the village and I'm alone on the mountain slope, among the wild flowers, the trees, the rocks.'

Because life was so busy, it was a few days before Isobel finished her letter. 'Let me tell you what homes here are like,' she wrote. 'The Lisu don't use furniture other than a raised plank of wood for a bed, rough cupboards and baskets to store grain. The people eat on the floor. One day we were sitting on the floor eating a meal with a family here in Pine Mountain village (now, isn't that a lovely name?), and a cat wove in and out between us as we ate, making odd dashes into the centre of the group to grab some food. Lucius, a Lisu Christian who was with us, put an end to her tricks. While we were eating, he held her tail down with his foot and she had to settle there till we finished!'

And that was not the only letter that was written. Having returned from their trip to Lisuland, John wrote to Mr. Fraser telling him that he was quite confident that they could cope with life in the mountains, and that they would love to go back there. That December, ten years after being called to minister to the Lisu, Isobel's dreams came true. But it was not long before she discovered how hard life in the mountains could be.

'I want Mummy,' Kathryn cried, not long after her parents had fallen asleep. 'I want Mummy.'

Isobel woke up, rose quickly, and picked up her distressed little daughter.

'Is she all right?' John asked sleepily.

'She's terribly hot.' Isobel peeled off some of the little girl's night clothes. 'Bring me some water and I'll sponge her over. That should bring her temperature down.'

But it didn't. And in the cool light of the following morning it was clear that Kathryn was really quite unwell.

'She must have caught a bug,' John said, looking at his pale little daughter. 'A day or two and she'll be better.'

Over the next few days Kathryn lost weight, grew listless, and just wanted to sleep. But as soon as she slept, her temperature rose and she cried herself awake again.

'We need help,' Isobel decided, having tried everything she could think of. 'I'm going to write to Dr. Haverson to ask his advice.'

The letter was written and a boy ran off with it. But that was just the first leg of its journey. There was no road and no regular postal service in the mountains. It was an anxious time for the Kuhns.

'I'm hungry,' a tiny voice beside her said. 'I want some rice.'

It was the middle of the night, and about ten days since Kathryn had fallen ill.

John hugged his little daughter while Isobel found some food. Even though it was pitch-black Isobel managed to rustle up some cold rice for Kathryn to eat. As Kathryn ate tiny mouthfuls, her parents thanked God for the beginnings of her recovery.

It was two months before a prompt reply to their letter came from Dr. Haverson!

Greetings and Goodbyes

Isobel Kuhn and Homay enjoyed each other's company from the first day they met.

'Tell me your story, Homay,' Isobel asked the young woman who sat on the mountainside with her. 'Tell me it right from the beginning. I've heard bits and pieces, but I'd like to hear it right through.'

Kathryn played with two little Lisu boys on the grassy slope beside them. Without taking her eyes off the children, Homay was too conscientious for that, she began her tale.

'My family started going to church when I was a girl,' she said. 'We were the first in the area to do that. But, when I was seventeen, my mother fell ill. My brothers said she was going to die because the demons were angry with us for believing in Jesus! My father prayed, but still Mum suffered terribly. Eventually Dad told my brothers to go for the wizard. I can't tell you how awful that felt.'

'What happened then?' Isobel asked.

'I had trusted in Jesus,' Homay said, 'and I wanted nothing to do with wizardry. So I ran away when he came. If I'd stayed at home I would have had to take part in the sacrifices and I wasn't going to do that. I went off as though I was looking for firewood, and I didn't come home until after the wizard had gone. My family were furious. I was beaten for what I did. Then, when my mother died and the wizard said it was because he'd been called in too late, they beat me over again because they thought the demons were angry because I was a Christian.'

'Were you often beaten at home?'

'Sometimes,' said Homay. 'After my family stopped going to church I used to go wood-gathering on Saturday nights so that I could go to the Christian meeting at Deer Pool Mountain. Then I'd stay there for the three services the next day. If my brothers found out about that they beat me and my husband joined in the beatings. But it was worth it,' she said defiantly.

'Your husband was just a boy when your father and his father agreed to your marriage, wasn't he?' Isobel asked.

'That's right. Then he came to live with us as a son of the family and to help with the work in the fields. That is our tradition. But as we grew up we disliked each other and were never even friends let alone husband and wife. Eventually he eloped with another girl. I thanked God for that, but my family were insulted. They had paid a lot of money for him. Our families had us divorced, but my father threatened to have me married to a non-Christian who, he said, would knock some sense into me.'

Homay's face was very serious as she spoke. Little Kathryn noticed that, ran to the young woman, gave her a hug, then raced off with her friends again. Homay smiled, then continued. 'Every day I went to a secret place and prayed to God that he would give me freedom to worship him, and that he would also provide me with a Christian husband. God always answers prayers, but sometimes we have to wait a while.'

'Very true,' agreed Isobel, thinking of the ten years between her call to work with the Lisu and her eventual arrival in Lisuland.

'That was when the new missionaries came. They were so kind. I was told me many things about Jesus and I started to learn to read. When it was time for them to leave, I was full of sadness. That was when she asked if I would think about cooking for the new missionary family who were coming, if I would be a servant to you.'

Isobel smiled. She knew this part of the story well, but wasn't going to stop Homay's account.

'You know what we Lisu are like,' Homay explained, 'we don't ever want to be servants, even if we are very poor. But the more I thought about it, the more it seemed to be an answer to my prayers. I thought I'd be able to worship with you, and learn more and more about Jesus. That's why I agreed to help the new missionary lady.' Homay blushed and smiled. 'I'm very glad I did,' she concluded.

Kathryn noticed Homay's smiling face, thought the smile was directed at her, and waved in response. Homay waved back.

'I remember the day we first met you,' said Isobel. 'We had just arrived, and having a servant wasn't even in my thoughts. Then you appeared with your bedding roll and you've been part of our family ever since.'

Not long after that conversation Homay came running to Isobel, her face flushed. Another young friend was with her. 'Homay's fiancé has arrived!'

Isobel looked up from bathing Kathryn, surprise written all over her face. 'I didn't know you were engaged to be married!' she said.

Drying the child quickly, Isobel went outside where she saw a shifty-looking young man, and one who wore the signs of the local religion.

'You can't marry him,' Isobel told the girl. 'It's not right for God's children to marry unbelievers.'

'But my family said "yes" to him a long time ago, after my husband was divorced from me.' Tears ran down Homay's face. 'What can I do Mrs. Kuhn?' she sobbed.

The young man went away and the subject was not raised again. But John and Isobel prayed for the safe-keeping of their little Christian sister. And Homay prayed for wisdom to know what to do.

'May I go home to visit my family?' Homay asked, some months later.

She was given permission, and prayed for.

'I wonder if she's been forced into marriage,' said John, after the girl had been away several weeks.

Isobel shook her head. 'I don't think so. She's gone through such a lot and stayed faithful to the Lord that I don't think she'll disobey his word now.'

Time passed and there was no news. A great sadness fell on the Kuhn household, as all three missed her so much.

'Ma-Ma!' Kathryn squealed with delight one sunny afternoon soon afterwards. 'Ma-Ma! Homay's come back!'

Isobel dropped her book and rushed to the front of the house. The girl looked tired and she was not her usual chatty self at all.

'Are things well with you?' Isobel asked.

Homay looked deep into Isobel's eyes. 'Things are well,' she said softly. 'I am free.'

Isobel was about to ask a question, but the girl's expression stopped the words coming.

'Please,' Homay said, 'please don't ask me about my time away. It has been difficult. My father is furious because he will have to pay money to the young man's family. I don't think I can ever go back again.'

Putting her arm round Homay's shoulders, Isobel guided her towards the house. 'God will reward you for this great suffering,' she said. Her heart ached for the pain the girl bore, but soared to heaven that a Lisu lass should be so strong in her faith, so determined to follow her Lord.

For over a year Homay lived with the Kuhns, learning to read and write, and to give talks about Jesus to the village children. When Isobel and her family went back to America on leave Homay said her sad farewells and a glad hello to her old friends.

'I will write a letter to Mrs. Kuhn,' Homay decided, one day some months later. She spent a long time writing it.

'You-who-have-gone-back-to-the-foreign-country, Ma-Pa, Ma-Ma, and Kathryn, whom I love, whom I never can forget, whom I deeply regard in Christ Jesus, whom I long to see. O dear, I think of you three and send you a handshake on paper. After we parted I wanted to see you, loved you, and many tears came out. Just after you left the landowner at Lu-mu-teh tried to hold up the building of the church. He put two of the Christians in jail on the Saturday. Early on Sunday, Mr. and Mrs. Cooke, the villagers and many others of us met before breakfast and prayed for them. God answered our prayers. Tuesday, towards evening, they were released, thank God!

By God's help I was enabled to walk all the way from Oak Flat to Luda in peace. Ma-Pa, Ma-Ma, you three, I would like to know if you arrived safely at the foreign country. Oh dear. Ma-Pa, Ma-Ma and Kathryn, I thank you; we lived together over a year and by God's grace during that time there was nothing happened to be regretted. I thank you. I learned how to study a little while I was with you, and learned how to do a few things. I am so sad. Oh dear, Ma-Pa, Ma-Ma and Kathryn I can't tell you how I long to see you and touch your hands a little, and take you, Kathryn, around a little. I can't forget your faces, it is as if I hear your voices in my sleep. Oh dear. When you get to your foreign country, don't forget us, but pray for us all the time. Thank you. Please forgive any mistakes I've made in writing this; thank you. The writer Homay Phoebe who loves you and will never forget you.'

When Homay wrote her letter, the Kuhns were in Canada.

'This is so strange,' Isobel said, as they travelled one day. 'We've been married for years, we have a dear little daughter, yet we've still to meet each other's families.'

John laughed. 'It has one advantage,' he teased.

'What's that?'

'They can't tell me they disapprove of my choice of a wife and forbid us to marry!'

Kathryn met her Grandfather Miller and her Grandmother and Grandfather Kuhn for the first time, and aunts and uncles and cousins too.

'When we've finished in America and Canada can we go to another country and meet more family there?' Kathryn asked one day.

John ruffled her hair fondly. 'I think you've met nearly everyone now,' he laughed, 'Apart, that is, from your uncle and aunt back in China.'

'I'm looking forward to going to school at Kunming with my cousin,' Kathryn said, excitedly.

Isobel's heart sank. She was longing to get back to Lisuland, but the thought of her little girl going off to school at Kunming was one she didn't allow herself to dwell on. She comforted herself with the thought that the Kuhn cousins would be together.

'I can't wait, I can't wait, I can't wait to get on the ship,' Kathryn sang, on the morning before they were due to leave. Her song continued, 'I'm going home, I'm going home to China!'

John looked at his wife who was pressing things into a suitcase. 'I can't wait either,' he said, 'but goodbyes are always so hard to say.'

'I know,' agreed Isobel, 'and it's not easy for our families either. The farewell service will be hard.'

Many of their friends and relations were in Vancouver for the occasion, which was a very bittersweet one. Having said their goodbyes, they went back to Isobel's father's home where they were to spend their last night in Canada. The phone rang as they entered.

'It's a call for you, John. It's the Mission secretary.' John took the phone and held it to his ear.

'I've just had a telegram saying that war has broken out between Japan and China,' the mission secretary said. 'I'm afraid all sailings must be delayed.'

'Then we don't go tomorrow?'

'Looks like it,' the Secretary agreed. 'Another missionary is already on the boat, she boarded at Seattle. I guess I'll have to cable her and tell her to get off here tomorrow. It really is too bad.'

After John had put the phone down, he turned to face Isobel and the few friends who had returned with them. Isobel had only heard half of the conversation and was very confused. Calling her by the pet-name he loved to use when speaking to his darling wife he reached out and held her hand, gently. 'We don't leave tomorrow, Belle,' he said quietly. 'China and Japan are at war. CIM is cancelling all passages.'

It was as though a damp cloud invaded the room. Isobel rose above it.

'But any fighting will be in the north, in Manchuria. That's the other side of China. Surely CIM missionaries in the south will be safe enough.'

'It's not our place to run the Mission,' said John. But his heart was not in what he was saying.

'That'll be a blanket order for the whole country,' Isobel insisted. 'They'll not have had time to think it through, to realise that we would be as far from the fighting as can be! And in the confusion of it all they've probably forgotten that Kathryn is going to the little school at Kunming rather than Chefoo. Now that would make a difference. Chefoo's right in the danger zone. If she were going there things would be entirely different.'

'We'll leave you to work this out,' the Kuhns' friends said. 'But remember, we'll take you to the ship if you're going.'

Having seen them to the door, John and Isobel returned to the sitting -room and looked at each other.

'Phone the secretary back and ask if we can still go,' Isobel suggested.

John reached for his Bible. 'We will ask the Lord first.'

Suddenly his eyes twinkled and his face broke into a smile. 'Guess you win, Belle. Our readings take us to Psalm 91 tonight, the psalm that promises protection in danger. Listen to this. "He who dwells in the shelter of the Most High will rest in the shadow of the Almighty. I will say of the Lord, 'He is my refuge and my fortress, my God, in whom I trust.' ... He will cover you with his feathers, and under his wings you will find refuge; his faithfulness will be your shield and rampart. You will not fear the terror of night, nor the arrow that flies by day... If you make the Most High your dwelling - even the Lord, who is my refuge - then no harm will befall you, no disaster will come near your tent...'

John reached for the phone. '..... So you see why we think we should still go,' he concluded, having told the Mission Secretary what God's Word had said.

'I've been thinking the very same thing,' Mr. Wilcox agreed. 'I was just about to call you. I'll get in touch with the Home Director and you'll hear from him one way or the other first thing in the morning.'

It was late but thet hardly slept that night. As soon as it was dawn their ears strained for the phone, but it was silent. At nine o'clock the news came. They could go!

It was 31st August, 1937. With Jack and Ella Graham and their two children, the Kuhn family left Vancouver on the *Hikawa Maru*, heading for Japan. They had been assured safe travel from Japan to Hong Kong then on to China. And the first two parts of their journey went well.

'Look!' John pointed to land in the distance, 'That's Hong Kong.'

Kathryn focused on the horizon. 'What date is it?' she asked.

'September 19th,' Isobel said. 'Why do you ask?'

Kathryn grinned. 'Because I'm counting the days.' John and Isobel looked at each other. So were they! 'And I'm looking forward to going to school at Kunming. It'll be nice to have two Kuhn girls together there!'

Her mother looked down. Yes, she thought, it will

be nice for you. And you'll be safe there at Kunming...
away from the fighting at Cheefoo at least. But how I'll
long for holiday times when we'll have our girlie home
with us.

'There's a telegram for you,' John was told, when
they berthed at Hong Kong. Isobel watched as he opened
it. 'What could it be?' she wondered.

John Kuhn's face stiffened. 'Send Kathryn to Chefoo
with Grace Liddell,' it read. The explanation was not long
in coming. A safe boat had been found that was going
from Hong Kong to Malaya, and CIM Headquarters
thought it was a good opportunity to get Kathryn to
Chefoo, the Mission school there, especially as a
missionary lady was to be travelling on the boat. The
whole situation was very confusing. The plan had been
to send Kathryn to Kunming, that had been the agreement
but here they were being told that she was now being
sent to Cheefoo. Hadn't the plan been to send Kathryn
to Kunming? Wouldn't that have been safer? Kunming
was further way from the fighting after all. Cheefoo,
though not in immediate danger, was a lot closer. Isobel's
heart ached. 'I'm not ready to say goodbye,' she said in a
small shocked voice. John's white face spoke volumes.

'It makes sense, Belle. She'll be fine with Grace.'

'But I'm not ready to say goodbye,' Isobel repeated.
'It's too soon.'

It was hard for them all, but the goodbyes were said.
Kathryn waved from the boat, half excited and half afraid.
Her mother's arm waved automatically, but her heart

was like lead within her. It was all so sudden, so confusing, not what had been planned at all. She went over and over in her mind the last time she had brushed Kathryn's hair, the last time she had bathed her, the last hug, the last kiss, until God made her realise what a useless thing she was doing. She learned a hard lesson in saying goodbye to little Kathryn.

'What a wonderful scene to welcome us,' John said, as they travelled on the last lap of their journey by train to Kunming, 6000 feet above sea level. Kathryn should have been with them, but she wasn't and another blow awaited the Kuhns on their arrival at Kunming. Isobel recorded it in her diary.

'Mr. Fraser told us today that we will be temporarily stationed at Paoshan with freedom to go to Lisuland on trips. He says he wants John as his assistant superintendent for West Yunnan.'

'It never occurred to me we'd not go straight back to our Lisu friends,' she complained to John that night.

'Belle,' John said patiently, 'we're not free agents. We go where God leads, and that is to Paoshan.'

'But..'

'There are no 'buts' in obeying our Father,' he said quietly but very firmly.

Four days later, Isobel had a day of private prayer during which she surrendered herself to the Lord's will. 'What joy and victory flooded me,' she told her husband later. She had learned another hard lesson.

'There's a letter from Mr. Fraser,' John Kuhn said,

just one month later. Slitting it open he read aloud, '.....I must ask you both to make a trip to Oak Flat. The church there is in trouble and someone who speaks the Lisu language is needed urgently. I would love to go myself but duties here don't allow it. You will escort a new Lisu missionary, Victor Christianson, who will stay at Oak Flat and learn the language. Remember,' the letter concluded, 'this is not a permanent posting. You don't need to take all your things with you, just enough for a few months. Having you there will be good for Victor.'

Isobel slipped out of the room to their bedroom and closed the door behind her. 'Temporary posting!' she laughed aloud, dancing round the room. 'Temporary posting! So says you, Mr Fraser. So says you!' Falling to her knees she poured out her worship, her praise and her thanksgiving to God, and all without words, so deep were her feelings.

Their 'temporary' stay in Lisuland began on December 13th 1937. They were still there the following September, though by then they were all packed up for a long trip to Burma.

'Here's a telegram,' a Lisu brother told John. Having read it, he handed it to his wife and to the new missionary, Victor. His face was grave. What they read rendered them speechless. 'Mr. Fraser is dead. He contracted malignant cerebral malaria and never recovered consciousness. The Superintendent has gone home to God. All missionaries will remain where they are stationed.'

47

Rainy Season Bible School

'I do miss Homay,' sighed Isobel. 'But what a wonderful experience she'll be having, away with the others to investigate the Bana area for the China Inland Mission. Imagine her excitement at travelling on a bus for the first time. Then the train ride - I can just picture her face when she saw a train!'

'What she will make of the city of Mandalay I really don't know,' Isobel thought. 'It couldn't be more different from here. But how wonderful it would be if CIM were able to work there. I'm sure God has great plans for Homay. This may help us to discern what they are.'

'The Bana mission party have returned!' a voice shouted one day. Everyone dropped what they were doing and ran to meet them.

'Homay!' Isobel called excitedly.

The plump little figure in the distance waved wildly, left the group, and ran into her friend's open arms.

'Are things well with you?' the missionary asked.

'Things are very well,' the girl assured her, eyes twinkling as she spoke. 'And Kathryn, what is the latest word of Little Sister?' Isboel loved to hear the sound of Homay's Lisu words... "Little Sister", "Big Brother",

"Third Sister", all these names and nick-names were part of the unique Lisuland vocabulary. Isobel took, her friend, Homay by the arm and, as they walked together up the mountainside to the village, she told her what Kathryn had written in her weekly letters.

Homay's eyes clouded. 'I will miss Little Sister,' she said. 'Your heart must be sad.'

'We knew it would be like this,' Isobel reminded her. 'And Kathryn writes such lovely letters. When I read them, I can almost hear her voice.'

Weeks later, Isobel wrote to a friend in Canada. 'When Homay returned from Bana, we found that she was too advanced for her old job as cook. She can now use the Lisu typewriter, and of the three locals who typed the Lisu New Testament manuscript, she was by far the best. She has become a sort of secretary to us and oversees the housekeeping, the buying in and measuring of grain, charcoal, salt, potatoes etc.Her afternoons are spent typing copies of the New Testament books for the Bible students. At the end of the month, when we gave her her small salary, she handed it back saying, "Ma-Pa, Ma-Ma, I would like to give the half of each day to working for the Lisu church by typing as my gift to God. I will do that for nothing. The other half of each day I will work for you, and for that I will take wages if this is agreeable to you." I thank God every day,' Isobel wrote, 'several times a day, for our dear Lisu friend and helper.'

'What other news have I?' Isobel wondered. Then a smile crossed her face. 'Of course, there's Victor our new missionary.' Picking up her pen, she wrote on.

'Although it broke our hearts to say farewell to dear Kathryn at Hong Kong, we did not return to Lisuland alone. Instead we brought with us Victor Christianson, a new CIM worker in the area. Let me tell you about him. Our first day's travelling was long and hard. It finished with a stiff rocky descent by feeble moonlight to a poor inn where we spent the night. Victor had to sleep in the only public room. I was in the next room and could hear everything that was happening. Lisu buildings are like that. I heard an old lady asking Victor what he was reading. Despite his tiredness he explained that it was God's Word. Then, in the gentlest and most patient of ways, he told her about the Lord Jesus. She had never heard of the Saviour, and might never hear of him again, so he told her all she needed to be saved. As I listened, I praised God for Victor. But, my dear friend,' she concluded, 'I'm as tired as Victor must have been that night, and the light is fading, so here I must end. God bless you, love, Isobel.'

Laying her pen down, Isobel stretched, reached for her Bible, and had her evening time with God.

'What's wrong?' Isobel asked, seeing John's shocked expression. He held a letter in his hand. It was a moment or two before he replied.

'Earl is dead,' he said.

Isobel sat down and read the letter for herself. She could hardly take in what she was reading. Their friend and colleague Earl Carlson was dead. It was an awful shock. Isobel looked up at John's tense face. Earl wasn't only their friend and colleague, he was loved and respected by all the Lisu Christians. It would be a shock to them also.

'I'll tell the congregation at the prayer meeting,' he said, 'that's a good time to tell them.'

The Lisu Christians knew right away that something had happened. John's normally happy expression was sombre. They gathered quietly for the meeting.

'Dear brothers and sisters,' John said, 'A letter came today. You know that the Lord brought Charles Peterson and Earl Carlson to Lisuland, to tell the people at Luda about the Lord?'

Heads nodded. The people wondered what was coming next. Had there been trouble at Luda? Was there another problem with drugs being grown?

'We've heard today,' John continued, choosing his words carefully, 'that Earl Carlson was smitten with typhus fever while working in the villages. A doctor was sent for, but arrived too late. The Lord has taken Earl Carlson home to himself. Charles Peterson saw his dear friend buried near the mission house. The Mission has decided to take Charles away from Luda for the time being, and to place him here in Oak Flat.'

Tears rolled down the faces of his listeners as a trembling voice began to sing. Others joined in, one by one: 'Safely, safely gathered in,
no more sorrow, no more sin,
God has saved from weary strife,
In its dawn, this young fresh life,
Which awaits us now above,

Resting in the Saviour's love.'

Lisu villagers watched the sorrowing little congregation, dignified in their grief as they sang.

'Jesus, grant that we may meet
There, adoring at Thy feet.'

'Why don't they wail and offer sacrifices to ward off the demons?' a villager asked wonderingly. 'They should call for the wizard, or the demons may bring typhus to them too.'

'I don't understand these Christians,' announced the first man, looking at the quiet little group which was gathered in prayer. 'They don't seem to fear death. They must be mad!'

'The Lisu evangelists are wonderful folk,' Victor said, when the missionaries met together one evening for prayer. He was settling into his new life and Charles Peterson was now the new person at the Oak Flat mission.

Charles agreed. 'The Lisu evangelists were a great help to me. No one could have been more caring than they were when Earl died. I just love them.'

Isobel agreed, thinking of her dear Lisu friends and what they meant to her.

'But we mustn't be sentimental,' John counselled. 'Their hearts are in the right place, are so enthusiastic that they put us to shame, but many are very ignorant about what the Bible teaches.'

Isobel nodded. 'You see,' she explained to the two

newcomers, 'as soon as they become Christians they start to tell others about the Lord. And such is their zeal to evangelise their fellow Lisu that they never stop talking about Jesus. In fact, they are so busy preaching and teaching that they don't have time to learn.'

'Which is why,' John chipped in, 'when we were on furlough we worked out a plan for a Rainy Season Bible School.'

'A what?' Victor and Charles said together.

Isobel explained their thinking. 'A full-time Bible School for the Lisu is impossible because no evangelism would be done. A day-release system won't work because of the distances involved.'

'Right enough,' Charles agreed. 'It takes four days to go from one end of our area to the other.'

Victor laughed. 'In other words, it could take an evangelist four days to get to a class, one day attending it and four days for the return journey. If we held classes each week, I reckon that he'd be studying for one, travelling for eight, and evangelising for minus two. That doesn't add up!'

'Which is why we thought of a Rainy Season Bible School,' said John. 'We've discovered in the past that it is dangerous for us to do much travelling in the rainy season.'

'We learned that the hard way,' Isobel interjected, 'when we were nearly washed away on several occasions, and when a house crashed down about our feet on another.'

'If we could collect our evangelists together in one

place for the rainy season, then no one would need to travel and put themselves at danger. The summer is out, our people have too much to do then to study. That's when they can travel, and when the Lisu take time to hear them.'

'Of course,' agreed Victor, 'That's when they leave the villages and camp beside the fields to protect their crops from birds and animals.'

'Which leaves the rainy season as the quiet time for evangelism and the perfect time for study.'

All heads nodded in agreement. So the Rainy Season Bible School (RSBS) was born.

'Darling Kathryn,' Isobel wrote in her weekly letter, in August 1938. 'What a busy day it has been, and what a happy one. Thomas, the evangelist, and Homay were married. Homay has had many sadnesses in her life because of the heathen marriage practices and because a Christian boy she loved was drowned. You were too young to understand these things at the time. But now your dear Homay is married to a good Christian man. She looked lovely in an outfit of orange silk and dark blue cotton. I played the Bridal March as they entered the church. But we are not losing her. They are going to live in the little house next to ours, and she will continue to work with us.'

Just over a year later, Kathryn wrote to Homay, having heard some news from her mother.
'Chefoo, October 1st, 1939.

My dearest Homay, I think of you and pray for you too. I cannot speak Lisu now except 'yes'. I hope you will teach me some Lisu when I see you again, because it is fun learning other languages.

Mummy has told me the secret that God told you, and I think it is a very nice secret. I will love the baby. I will tell you a name if it is a girl - Kathryn - not because it's my name, but because it means 'the gift of God', and if it is a boy - John - that is only to help you.

I love you very much.

I am having a good time at school, and am learning very much. It is only 28 days till the holidays.

With love from Kathryn K.'

Letters went weekly from Chefoo to Lisuland and from Lisuland to Chefoo, but John and Isobel longed to see their little daughter again face to face.

'The news is not good,' John said to his wife, when they were discussing the war situation in 1940. 'The Mission is quite right not allowing the Chefoo children to travel this holiday. They'll be much safer where they are.'

His wife nodded in agreement. She didn't trust herself to speak.

Although the war rumbled on in the distance during 1940 and 1941, there were troubles of a different kind in Lisuland.

A young Lisu boy ran up to John, frightened and anxious. 'What's that noise?' he asked John.

Seeing the boy's frightened expression, John stopped

what he was doing and they went outside together.

'Look Ma-Pa! There is smoke in this direction and in that direction too,' The young Lisu boy pointed to both the north and the south. 'The earthquake is going to come to our village. The evangelist Big Brother is in Sandalwood Flat and look at the smoke coming from there!' The young boys voice rose in alarm. But John's calm and sensible nature calmed him down.

'The Lord who made the earth holds it in his hands,' John assured the boy. 'Whatever happens, we are safe in the arms of Jesus.'

Suddenly, the earth shook violently and a noise like the crash of many thunders filled the air. John fell to his knees in prayer. The boy, shaking, did the same. Christians all over the village held Lisuland up in prayer till the roarings and rumblings stopped several hours later.

'Ma-Pa! Ma-Pa!' A voice called in the afternoon of the following day. It was Big Brother. John and his young friend, who was trembling with relief at seeing him again, ran out to meet the Lisu evangelist.

'What happened? Are you hurt? Is the Christian village still there? Was anyone killed?'

'You're not giving him time to answer,' John Kuhn said. 'Let Big Brother sit down and tell us his story.'

By then a group had gathered round them. John led them to the church where they heard what the young man had to say.

'I was visiting the Christians at Sandalwood Flat when the earthquake struck,' Big Brother told his audience. 'I was on the trail, just about to start the journey home, when there was a mighty landslide. A man was hoeing a field about 500 feet beneath us at the time.'

More people came in, non-Christians among them. Big Brother had to speak louder to be heard.

'A huge slice of our mountain shot off when the earth quaked. We yelled to the man, but he had no time to escape. He raised his arms as if calling for help, then he was buried in rock. The whole ridge landed on top of him, and the earth around that place is still loose and sliding. There is a big crack in the Crown Rock at Sandalwood, and inside the crack the mountain is rumbling and sending out billows of smoke. What is inside a mountain that makes it smoke?' Big Brother asked.

'It's a dragon that does it,' one of the non-Christians said.

Another added. 'When he turns over the mountain shakes.'

'Go on with your story,' John prompted, being more interested in what had happened than in either geology or dragons.

'That's all I know,' Big Brother said. 'My froemd Lu-seng was out preaching, but I didn't see him after the earthquake.'

'I told you so,' one of his listeners said. 'The dragon came out of the mountain and ate him.'

Several others agreed with him. We'll not see Lu-seng again, they decided.

'I think you will.' It was John Kuhn who spoke,

for he had just seen Lu-seng come in the door of the church. The Christians burst into praise. Their friend was safe and sound! Silence fell as he started to speak, telling the same story they had heard from Big Brother.

'About forty were killed, I think,' he concluded. 'But all of the Christians are safe.'

'The gods were judging us for our sins,' one of the non-Christian Lisu said.

'That's why no Christians were killed,' suggested another.

John stood at the front of the church and told them about Jesus. 'You see,' he said as he drew to a close, 'even if Christians had been killed, they would have gone to heaven because their sins have been forgiven. And God will forgive your sins too if you trust in the Lord Jesus Christ.'

Some Lisu stayed to hear more. Others walked away muttering something about angry dragons.

No sooner had talk about the earthquake died down, when talk about opium taxes began. The Lisu Christians discussed the situation in depth.

'The Opium Commissioner is at Luchang. He's demanding the tax from Christians even though it's against church rules to grow opium.'

There was much discussion about this.

'He's threatening to drive away the cattle belonging to any believers who don't pay.'

'We must pray about it.'

'We'll know what to do when the deacons come back from Rainy Season Bible School on Monday.'

'Yes, they will know what to do.'

'We are agreed on our three decisions?' one deacon asked, as he brought the Monday meeting to a close. All heads nodded in agreement.

'First,' he said, 'we'll pay the tax even though we don't grow opium. Second, we'll ask Ma-Ma to write and appeal to the President of China in the name of the Lisu church. Third, we'll have a day of prayer and fasting on Sunday 8th June.'

But Friday came first. And on Friday Homay died. Tears in his eyes, and baby John tied to his back, Thomas was being comforted by the Christians in his shanty.

'Homay is at peace now,' one of the deacons said. Thomas wiped tears from his eyes.

'I know that. She is with Jesus.'

'You can have my coffin,' a fellow Christian offered. 'I can have another one made.'

'Thank you,' the widower said. 'That is very kind of you. It would take three days to have one made.'

Through red and swollen eyes, Thomas looked at Homay's body. 'She seems so peaceful, but she was only thirty,' he wept.

I Have Two Ears, Ma-ma

'The situation is very serious, Belle,' John said.

Isobel agreed. 'Who would have thought at the beginning of 1941, that it would be like this before the end of the year.'

'I think you should write a prayer letter to our friends at home. We need all the prayer support we can get.'

'I'll certainly do that,' Isobel agreed. 'But how much background knowledge can we assume our friends in Canada and America have?'

John thought about that. 'None at all,' he decided, 'because we've no idea how much information gets through in wartime. But you'll have to be careful what you write.'

'I'll just state the bald facts, and I'll make it brief.'

'That would be best.'

'The war between China and Japan has been going on for years,' Isobel wrote to their supporters, 'but it was mostly in the north, in Manchuria. Until now it has just seemed like distant rumblings to us. However, things are changing. A little while ago the Japanese entered Burma, and walked through that small land as though they were wearing seven-league boots. Our work is right on the China-Burma border, north of the Burma Road. It is our prayer that they will come no further. You see,' she explained, 'they will be anxious to capture the Burma Road, because that is how supplies come into China. If the Japanese army controls the road, it controls the country. Please pray.'

At the end of the year a letter came from CIM Headquarters.

'I've been called to a conference at Chungking.' John looked up from the letter. 'Will you be safe here or would you be better coming with me?'

'Nowhere in China is safe,' Isobel replied. 'And the work needs to go on. How long will the conference last?'

John shook his head. 'I don't know. But I won't be away any longer than I need to be. Will you be all right here?'

Isobel nodded. She didn't have Homay anymore but she did have Lucius, her replacement. A kind and capable man who would do anything for her. She looked up at John and smiled.

'Yes, I'll be fine. When you're away our friend Lucius looks after me like a mother hen... but remember he gets married soon... then he moves out to make a home of his own.'

Her husband laughed. 'I'll be back before Lucius is married, and I'll take over the clucking!'

'It won't be the same when he moves over the river,' Isobel said. 'He's become almost as much part of the family as Homay was.'

'You still miss her, don't you?' asked John tenderly.

'She was like a sister to me,' his wife conceded. 'I think about her every day.'

'And I'll think about you every day while I'm away.'

Isobel laughed. 'And if you're good, I'll count the days until you come home.'

Shortly after John left, the first month-long Bible School for girls was held.

'A Bible School for girls!' some of the men laughed when the idea was first suggested. Despite their doubts about it, the men had listened carefully to Isobel's suggestions none the less.

'Not everyone is invited,' she had told them, 'only those who fulfil these rules of admission.'

1. The girl student must be a saved Christian, not just a professing one.

2. She must have a recommendation from the deacon of her village that for the past year at least her conduct has been irreproachable.

3. She much be able to read and write.

4. She must be at least seventeen years old; no limit after that.'

'Women have not the brains to learn things,' said one man, then remembered his missionary teacher was a woman!

'Only six girls have signed up,' one Lisu evangelist told Isobel, in the last week of January. 'But don't be discouraged, more than that intend to come.'

'I've no idea how many will turn up,' she wrote in her diary. 'But however many come, it will still be worthwhile.'

'There are eighteen here now,' Lucius said, 'but they are so giggly that they'll not hear a thing.'

Girls came a day's journey from the north, and from the south, and some came from the other side of the river.

'The blind girl, Leah, has come from the village of Deer Pool,' one of the students said. 'Look, her friend is guiding her along the road.'

Isboel smiled, in welcome, as the blind girl's young friend spoke to her, slightly nervously.

'Ma-Ma, the rules are that students must be able to read and write. Leah used to be able to read, but her eyes don't see so well now. Would you allow her to come and listen?'

'Of course!' Isobel said brightly, giving the girl a warm hug. Leah's face beamed with happiness.

'Why do you want to study at the school?' Isobel asked Leah later.

'Because I want to know the Bible better. I've not been able to read it for some time now.'

The missionary smiled. 'If I can help in any way, just ask,' she said.

'Ma-Ma,' Leah said, 'I'm told that the girls' school is to be just like the RSBS.'

'Yes, we are going to try to do just the same here as we do there.'

'Then there will be weekend preaching assignments for us each week?'

'That's the plan, but ….'

'Ma-Ma, I'd like to ask a favour. When you send me out, could you please send me with one of my friends? I can see a little bit, but I can't walk quickly over strange trails. My friends are used to that and don't mind taking me by the hand.'

Tears filled Isobel's eyes. She told John about it in a letter. 'I'd not thought of sending a blind girl out over these high and dangerous paths, but her courage shamed me. If she is willing to go, who am I to say it's too much for her?'

On the last night of February, Isobel wrote another letter to her faraway husband. '24 girls came, and two were not accepted. But the 22 who remained did so well. We held tests and gave out certificates to those who passed. The results were good. One even got first-class honours. And who do you think she was? The blind girl, Leah! She had exactly the same exam questions as the others, only we took hers orally. The girls had written down notes from which to revise; she had none. Part of the exam was recitation of Scripture passages, and Leah could not read, yet she did best of all. I asked her how she did it. Her face glowed with pleased embarrassment as she answered, "Well, I could hear the other girls in my hut going over their notes and the scripture as they studied for the exam and I studied by listening to them.'

We had a service to finish with to which some boys from the RSBS came along, ostensibly to escort their sisters home, but I think it was really to see if the girls had learned anything at all. At the end of the service one of these lads exclaimed with beaming face, "Why, wasn't that nice! It was almost as good as ours." Complacent male! I thought it was every bit as good.'

It was good when visitors came and one day Isobel heard the latest news from their missionary friend and his wife James and Elizabeth Brown. 'Yunnan, Kweichow and Szechwan are the only three provinces left to China,' James told Isobel. 'On the way here we heard that Generalissimo Chiang has just lost another province.'

'We are very much in the firing line now,' Isobel said. 'I'm not sure how long we'll be safe here.'

'What about Kathryn?' Elizabeth Brown asked. 'She's at Chefoo?'

Isobel swallowed hard before answering. 'Have you heard the news about Chefoo?' Elizabeth shook her head. 'The school has been captured by the Japanese. Our little girlie is wrapped in silence. I miss her weekly letters so much. Just occasionally a tiny note gets through to me. It's only because of them I know she's alive. At least,' Isobel finished in a whisper, 'at least I know she was alive when her last letter was written. I don't know how she is now.'

Elizabeth looked shocked. 'And John went away and left you to carry that burden?'

Seeing her guests' reaction, Isobel became her matter-of-fact self and explained. 'That's not how it was at all. John was at a superintendents' conference when Chefoo fell. He had no idea that was going to happen when he left. And he had intended being back by now, however, circumstances beyond his control have prevented his return. But don't worry, Elizabeth, he'll be back just as soon as he can be.'

'You're all alone here?' James asked.

Isobel laughed. 'No one is ever alone in China! And our Lisu brothers and sisters in Christ care for me beautifully. Lucius, he's the lad you met when you arrived, is like a son to me.'

'Are you sure you should stay?'

'Oh yes,' was the firm reply. 'I'm sure. Do you think I would leave here, and perhaps miss a letter from Kathryn?'

Some weeks later another letter arrived, but it was not from Kathryn.

'You look sad, Ma-Ma,' said Lucius.

Isobel had just reread the letter.

'Is it bad news of Little Sister Kathryn?'

'No. It's not. But it's rather difficult to explain.'

'I have two ears, Ma-Ma, and I will use both of them to listen to what you say.'

How fortunate I am, thought Isobel. And who could refuse such an offer.

'Sit down, Lucius, and I will tell you what this letter is about. Can you imagine what it is like to be on the opposite side of the world from your family?'

'No, Ma-Ma. I can't imagine what it would be like to be two mountains away. But I will try.'

'Ma-Pa and I have family in Canada and America, but

not all of them write to us with their news. Most write to our friend, Mary Zimmerman, and she sends us long letters which tell us all the family news.'

'Ma-Ma Zimmerman is then a real friend.'

Isobel smiled. It was beautiful that because Mary was her friend she was immediately accepted as Ma-Ma. How kind this boy is, thought Isobel.

'But Ma-Ma Zimmerman's mother has died, and my friend is in deep sorrow with that and other troubles.'

'For her mother to die is deep enough sorrow without other troubles too,' sympathised Lucius. 'Your letter is from Ma-Ma Zimmerman?'

'No,' the missionary explained. 'It is a letter from another friend saying that Ma-Ma Zimmerman will not be able to write to me for some months. She needs time to recover, time to herself.'

'The Lisu never need time to themselves, but white people do. When we are in deep sorrow we need everyone with us. But does your friend's troubles mean that you won't hear from your family?'

'I'm afraid it does.'

'Then I can imagine how it feels to be at the other side of the world,' the young man said. 'It must feel like being alone.'

'Lord,' Isobel prayed that night, 'I'm confused. You've made me to be a mothering person but all my 'children' are being taken from me. John is away for months yet. Only you know what is happening to Kathryn. Homay's with you, though I still long for her company. All my 'girls' are away home to their villages. And even Lucius has moved across the river to set up home now that he's married.'

As she spoke, it was as though she knew what God was saying to her. 'You have me. You're not alone. Even if you lose everyone, you're still not alone. Perhaps now that your loved ones are not all around you, you'll think more about me.'

Isobel wanted to argue that he should not have made her motherly if he was going to take away all the people she cared about. But she stopped short, remembering what the Lord had done for her.

'Precious Jesus,' she prayed, 'help me to bear it.'

In the Firing-line

Isobel's painful moaning woke her once again. She got up, dressed, and sat down to think. 'I can't bear this toothache any longer,' she decided. 'It's not going to go away, and it's driving me out of my mind.'

'Ma-Ma, you are ill?' a Lisu friend asked, seeing Isobel's white face and sleepless eyes.

'No, not ill. I have bad toothache. There is a dentist at Kunming, he'll be able to help me.'

'But Kunming is thirty days away!'

Isobel smiled despite the pain. 'No, the Burma Road means that the journey should only take two weeks. I'll be back within the month.' Isobel's smile hid real concern. 'How will I cope with this ripping pain for two weeks?' she wondered.

'But Ma-Ma, the Burma Road is dangerous. There is news of soldiers and shooting every day.'

Isobel said soothingly, 'God will go with me. And I have the beginnings of an idea ...'

'Some ideas are good and some are very bad,' the Lisu woman said. 'This war fills my head with bad ideas.'

'Mine is the very best of ideas. Ma-Pa is in Chungking at the Conference. He and I could meet up at Kunming and we could return to Oak Flat together.'

The Lisu woman's face lit up and she clapped her hands in excitement. 'Then everything will be all right,' she said. 'And when you come back here with Ma-Pa, everything will be all right here too!' Despite the searing pain, Isobel smiled.

'Lord,' Isobel prayed the night before leaving Oak Flat, please keep us safe on this journey. May your angels guard us as we travel.'

It was still very early in the morning when the porters were packed and everyone was ready to go.

'Ma-Ma!' a voice said, through the morning mist. 'I will escort you to Paoshan.' By the end of this announcement, Lucius was beside Isobel, and before she could argue with him, he had helped her on to her mule. 'I heard you were travelling to Kunming and the Lord told me you needed me.'

'I asked God to send his angels to care for me, and he sent you, an angel indeed.'

Lucius laughed. 'Do angels need nails?' he asked.

Isobel looked down from the mule into the sparkling eyes of her Lisu companion. 'I can't think of a verse that tells us they do,' she admitted.

'My new home needs nails to hold it together, and I will get them at Paoshan,' the young man said. 'God has planned this, I'm sure.'

'We've done 30 miles,' Isobel wrote in her diary that night. 'Lucius has chattered the whole way. And God has dulled my toothache! We are camping tonight in a big airy loft over a horse stable.'

When they reached the motor road, Isobel and Lucius got a lift from two American airmen. Four-and-a-half days after leaving Oak Flat, they arrived at Paoshan.

'I'm so tired,' Isobel groaned, as she got up at four the next morning, 'but I need a quiet time before we travel.' She read Genesis 28. Verse 15 seemed to spring out of the page. 'I am with you and will watch over you wherever you go, and I will bring you back to this land. I will not leave you until I have done what I have promised.'

'This is God's word for me,' Isobel said aloud. 'Thank you, Lord, thank you.'

'See this Lucius,' she said, pointing to the verse, when he came in to rope up her bedding for the next part of her journey. 'God has reminded me that he'll be with me and that he'll keep me.'

The young man read what it said and his face lit up. 'Ma-Ma, look! He says he will bring you back again too!'

It had never occurred to Isobel that she might not return. The two said goodbye to each other as Isobel climbed into the Americans' car.

Having a lady missionary with them rather cramped the young men's style, but most of the time they were kind enough. Four days into their journey, the car broke down.

'What do we do now?' one asked the other.

'I'll hold up the next truck that passes at gunpoint,' his friend replied. 'We can't talk Chinese, but we can talk gun.'

Isobel was appalled. 'Don't do that,' she pleaded. 'I speak Chinese. I can interpret for you.'

An hour, and several uncomfortable experiences later, a white man in a jeep picked them up. Because there was no room for luggage, Isobel had to travel on with nothing but what she wore and could carry in her little bag.

'I can't wait to see the family,' she thought as her nine day journey neared its end. Isobel was looking forward to meeting up with John's sister and her husband. Kathryn had been named after John's sister, now married and named Kathryn Harrison.

'It will be so good to see John's sister and her husband here. Kathryn and David will look after me. I don't think I could cope without them.' Isobel thought anxiously.

On 27th March 1942, tired, lonely and ill, Isobel pushed open the gate of the China Inland Mission's guesthouse in Kunming.

'Is anybody there?' she called.

All was silent. Entering the house with sinking heart, Isobel called out again. 'Is there anybody there?'

Eva, a young Chinese woman, greeted her. 'The Harrisons are not at home. But come in. I will take care of you.'

Isobel was grateful to sit down in safety and comfort, but disappointed not to see the family.

'You are ill?' Eva asked, looking at her visitor.

Isobel nodded. 'I need to see a dentist, perhaps a doctor. My toothache has gone, but you are right, I'm ill.'

The source of Isobel's trouble could not be found, and she grew weaker and more and more unwell.

'I'm really worried about Mrs. Kuhn,' the doctor told Eva. 'When will the Harrisons be back?'

'I don't know exactly,' the girl replied, 'but soon.'

The man paced up and down the room then came to a decision. 'I'm going to send a telegram to her husband. I think he should come right away. She is sinking fast.'

Eva's face drained of colour. As soon as the doctor left, she knelt down and poured out her heart to the Lord. Her prayers were answered when the Harrisons returned. And on 5th April John Kuhn flew to Kunming.

The next few days saw no improvement in Isobel's condition. Things were at their bleakest when at last a diagnosis was made. What had began as toothache ended as gangrene. With appropriate treatment, she slowly began to regain her strength.

'I think I've been very ill,' she confided in John. 'And Eva has nursed me like a baby.'

'I know that.' He squeezed her hand. 'The doctor said that another twenty-four hours and you would have died. Thank God they found out what was wrong.'

His wife closed her eyes and thought of her own little Kathryn who could so easily have been motherless.

'What's that noise?' Isobel asked a week later, as she woke from restful sleep.

John was on his knees in prayer at the side of the bed. 'It's an air-raid alarm. The Japanese have taken Lashio.'

Isobel was immediately wide-awake. 'But you would have been there had you not been called to be with me.'

'Yes,' he nodded grimly. He was thinking of those who were still there. 'Belle, I'll have to go and warn the isolated missionaries. They may not be aware of the danger. I should only be away a few days.'

It was with a heavy heart she watched him go, and with a heavier heart that she wrote her diary seven days later.

'Paoshan has fallen to the Japanese. The carnage is terrible. 15,000 are estimated killed. Survivors are stampeding on to the Burma Road. John is somewhere in the middle of it all.'

On May 9th, John Kuhn arrived back in Kunming, in the company of a group of missionaries. They had only just escaped with their lives. Four days later he left again, this time to warn the missionaries in Tali of the danger.

'Ladies, you are being quite unreasonable,' the British Consul official insisted. 'You really must leave on the RAF convoy tomorrow. The Japanese have crossed the Salween and they're on the Burma Road.'

Kathryn Harrison and Isobel wished their husbands were there to help them decide. What should they do? After the Consul's third communication in one day, they decided to go. Kathryn Harrison, her little son Charlie Harrison, Isobel, Eva and another lady missionary climbed aboard an army truck, and the convoy began to move. Seven days and seven nights of travel gave Isobel plenty of time to think. She thought of John, her husband who was somewhere in Yunnan, and then she thought of her own little daughter, Kathryn, who was being held captive by the Japanese at Chefoo.

'God said he would be with me,' Isobel thought to herself, 'he promised the day I left Paoshan.' Suddenly her face lit up and a smile smoothed her troubled features. 'And he said he would take me back! Praise the Lord!' her heart sang. 'Thank you, God. I know you'll keep your promise.' Wedged between a typewriter and the truck's spare tyre, Isobel felt a peace that she'd not known for some time.

'We're looking for Mrs. Kuhn and Mrs. Harrison,' a man's voice said, when the convoy stopped at Suyung, six days after leaving Kunming. I have a telegram from their Mission Headquarters.'

Kathryn Harrison got hold of the telegram and tore it open. As she did so, Isobel prayed. What news would it bring? Kathryn read aloud, 'Get off convoy at Luhsien in Szechwan Province. Stay with Mr. and Mrs. Lea until further notice.'

The two women looked at each other. 'We'll get to Luhsien tomorrow, Isobel said. 'And I won't be sorry to get off this truck. I've been leaning against that typewriter so long I think I've got the alphabet embossed on my back!'

Her sister-in-law laughed. 'And I don't think I'll ever hear the words spare tyre again but I'll think of being jammed up against one for nearly a week!'

'Welcome to Luhsien!' their host in Luhsien, Mr. Lea, waved at the weary travellers as they climbed down from their trucks. 'We are so glad to see you.' Hands were shaken all round the group.

'Has Yunnan Province fallen to the Japanese?' Isobel asked, as they set off for the mission house.

Mr. Lea registered surprise at the thought. 'No,' he assured her, 'the war news is good these last few days. Generalissimo Chiang's best regiment chased the enemy back over the Salween River. Yunnan was saved from invasion.'

'Why did God bring us here when there was no real danger?' Kathryn Harrison wondered aloud.

Arnold smiled. 'Perhaps it was to give you good news about Chefoo.' Isobel's eyes opened wide. 'We've just heard that the school is safe. The children are being kindly cared for by their captors.'

Two tears escaped from Isobel's eyes and trickled down her cheeks. 'Thank God,' she whispered, 'Thank God.'

There was a lot of thinking to be done that evening.

'We've no way of getting back to Yunnan,' Kathryn Harrison decided.

'And no money either,' her sister-in-law pointed out. 'So what does God want us here for?'

Mr. Lea had a suggestion. 'For the mean time I think you should brush up on your Chinese and help with the church work here.'

Isobel smiled. 'The last time I used my Chinese was

to stop two Americans shooting their way out of a breakdown.' Mrs. Lea's eyebrows arched. Isobel yawned. 'I'll tell you that story tomorrow!'

Return to Lisuland

Isobel read the paragraph in John's letter for the twentieth time. 'It's hard going working with the Medical Unit here in Paoshan. Cholera broke out after the terrible bombing so we are inoculating the refugees, hundreds and hundreds of them! We hear such stories from them. Their hearts are bruised and broken, just longing for comfort, but not knowing that it can only be had in Jesus. I wish you were here with me, Belle. There is so much you could be doing.'

'Can't I go back?' Isobel asked Mr. Lea.

'That would be most unwise,' he replied. 'Remember, it was the British Consul who sent you here, and I don't see him agreeing to your returning yet. They're still fighting in Yunnan. In any case, the trucks are bringing people out, not taking anyone back in!'

'I don't understand what's happening,' Isobel told the Lord. 'You promised that I would get back home again, and I'm stuck here. There's work for me to do in Paoshan.'

Even after praying about it, Isobel had no peace of heart. 'I'll write to the Mission's Director tomorrow,' she decided, before going to bed but before the Director's reply had time to arrive another letter told Isobel that there was no reason why she shouldn't return. Isobel was more unsettled than ever.

June 13th 1942 dawned like any other day, but the sun shone on Isobel's heart when her reply came from Mission Headquarters. 'I advise you to remain where you are until John invites you to return,' was the Director's advice.

Her head spun. She remembered John's last letter and wondered, 'Does "I wish you were with me" equal inviting me back to Yunnan?' Her heart told her it did, but her head was not sure.

Pouring her heart out to Kathryn Harrison Isobel sighed, 'I desperately want to go back right now, but is that what God wants?'

Kathryn listened attentively and thought before answering. 'Pray about it, Belle,' she counselled. 'You've asked the Director, you've asked Mr Lea, you've asked me. Set aside a time and place to ask God ... and wait for his answer.'

Isobel hugged her sister-in-law. 'Thank you. You're a really good friend. I'll spend Sunday in prayer and fasting.'

The following Sunday morning, Isobel took herself out to the Chinese cemetery where she could be sure of peace and quiet. There she made a list before the Lord of the things she felt she needed in order to return.

1 Money to pay for the trip

2 A clear invitation from John

3 A truck going to Yunnan

4 A companion to go with her

'I just can't believe it!' she told Kathryn Harrison excitedly. 'Yesterday I made four requests to God. Today, all four are answered. What could be clearer than that?'

'Tell me it all again,' her sister-in-law laughed. 'I can hardly take it in!'

Isobel sat down and held up one finger. 'First was the cable from John, urging me to go back right away.' A second finger rose. 'Then Mr. Lea heard about the convoy of merchant trucks going to Kunming.' She held up finger number three. 'Not long after that, your friend Eva, asked if she could go with me. But the money, that was the most amazing of all. It's years since we gave our friend a loan of $100. I'd forgotten all about it. And to think that the girl sent it in two repayments of $50, six months apart, and that they both arrived here today and together! I'll never, ever forget this answer to prayer.'

'I won't either,' agreed Kathryn Harrison. 'It's amazing.'

'You know,' Mr. Lea said, 'some poor souls would say it was just coincidence.'

Isobel shook her head. 'I think it takes more blind faith to believe such things are coincidence than it does to believe that they are God's answers to prayer!'

Just days later, Isobel Kuhn and Eva, set out on the first part of their journey. This was to take them to Kunming, where they hoped to meet up with Kathryn's husband David who was still working there.

'Welcome back to Kunming!' Dave Harrison said warmly. 'Come and make yourselves at home.'

Eva did. Within minutes she was in the kitchen, and before long appetising smells wafted through to the others.

'I can't wait to get to John,' Isobel said, as they ate their meal. David didn't respond.

'Is there something wrong?'

'No, not at all,' he assured Isobel. 'I just wondered if you could stay here and teach English for a couple of weeks until I come home from my next trip.'

Isobel swallowed hard before writing her thoughts in her diary that night. 'I don't want to stay. I want to get back to John. I just long to feel his arms around me. But it seems to be God's will for me to stay till David comes back. So be it.'

And she was glad she did, for one of her students became a Christian.

'Mr. Harrison will be home tomorrow,' said Eva.

Isobel smiled. 'I know. I've been counting the days. As soon as I arrive at Tali I will see John, and we leave the day after tomorrow. It's two months now since we saw each other.'

But that was not to be. On arrival at Tali, the news was that John was away with the Medical Unit. He would not be back for four weeks!

'I will make you a lovely meal,' Eva said comfortingly. There was no response. 'You will enjoy it.'

Isobel nodded. 'Thank you,' she whispered, afraid to speak in case her voice broke.

'Ma-Ma!' called Eva less than an hour later. 'A letter has come for you.'

Isobel looked at the handwriting and the sadness melted from her face.

'It's from my girlie!'

Opening the envelope slowly, she savoured the feeling of anticipation. Although Eva left the room she stayed within earshot in case the news was not good. But all she heard was silence. When the meal was cooked, Eva took it in.

'Dinner Ma-Ma.'

'Thank you,' said Isobel, without disturbing the smile on her face.

Eva looked at the missionary and thought how lovely she looked.

'Kathryn is very well. She's happy and she's safe. Although all the Chefoo children are in an internment camp, they are being kindly looked after.'

It didn't bother Eva at all that Ma-Ma hardly noticed the meal she had cooked for her.

'That's the first letter I've had in seven months. And in wartime seven months feels like forever.'

Her companion nodded. Isobel had finished her meal. She was still smiling when Eva removed the dirty dishes.

On August 4th Isobel's joy was complete. John arrived in Tali, and they were lost in each other's arms.

'How will we ever get to Oak Flat?' Isobel asked her husband. 'We can't leave here without permission from the military.'

John laughed. 'Thinking of your beloved Lisuland as

usual! Well, I don't know the answer to your question, but God does.'

And it wasn't long before the Kuhns knew too.

'The Colonel is providing us with an escort right back to the village?' questioned Isobel.

'That's what he said.'

'When?'

'We've to be ready tomorrow!'

Isobel was on her feet like a flash. 'Eva!' she called. 'Eva! We need to pack.'

Suddenly she realised how little they had. 'It's all right,' she grinned when her companion rushed through the door. 'We're leaving tomorrow for Lisuland, but we can pack all we have in twenty minutes.'

'What driving,' Isobel whispered to Eva, as the truck they were in hurtled along the Burma Road.

'I'm praying, Ma-Ma,' a frightened voice replied. 'Does the driver not see there are bends on the road and a sheer drop beside it?'

They careered along, tearing round the hairpin bends. Suddenly there was a screech. The truck swayed from side to side, it seemed to be dragging and bouncing at the same time, and keeling over as it went.

'Jump! Belle! Jump!' It was John's voice she heard above the screams.

She grabbed for the side of the truck, only the precipice was beneath her. The driver struggled to regain control. The vehicle swayed and lurched to the other side of the road. Grabbing Eva, Isobel thrust open the cab door and jumped.

Soldiers lay everywhere, heads gashed open, bloody and moaning. John came running, followed by the Colonel and a doctor who was with them.

'Are you all right?' John asked anxiously. Isobel nodded.

'Boil water!' ordered the doctor.

Eva ran up the hillside, scrabbling for twigs as she went. Isobel washed wounds and helped where a doctor wasn't urgently needed.

'Ma-Ma,' said Eva's voice shakily. 'Look.' She pointed down the precipice to the wreck of what had been an army truck, wedged a hundred feet below where they stood.

'It's a miracle we're not down there too.'

Darkness fell as the last casualty was seen to. There was nothing for it but to stay there on the mountainside overnight. John wrapped his wife and Eva in his coat and the two women huddled close to each other for warmth and comfort.

'Ma-Ma, God saved our lives today.'

Isobel nodded. 'That's because he still has work for us to do. And I believe he promised to take me safely back to my dear Lisu people.'

'I'm glad I was in your truck then, Ma-Ma.'

Isobel smiled for the first time since their hair-raising experience. 'That's right, Eva. You and I will stick close together.'

They didn't sleep well and were relieved when morning came.

'The Colonel says we have to go back by Paoshan,' John told the women.

Isobel shook her head. 'Another delay!'

'But Ma-Ma, we'll be able to buy flour and sugar to take with us.'

'You're quite right Eva. Let's work out all we need.'

But things weren't what they had expected when they arrived in Paoshan.

'It's deathly quiet,' Isobel said in a whisper, as if her voice would disturb the silence.

'It's the quietness of death.'

She looked around in disbelief. 'It's been bombed flat. How did anyone survive?'

'One of the believers escaped by crawling into a culvert under the main street when the bombs fell,' John told her.

'And the others? Did many of our brothers and sisters perish?'

'No,' John assured her. 'Only one. He was paralytic and could not run to safety. And now he's safe forever with the Lord.'

There was a long silence as each thought their own thoughts in the face of the devastation they saw around them.

'I understand now why you had to stay here.'

John nodded grimly. 'If we hadn't inoculated the survivors, those who escaped the bombs would have died of cholera.'

His wife looked round about her. 'I see that,' she said. 'I see that now.'

A few days later, the Kuhns were back in Lisuland, back in Oak Flat village.

'I should be so happy,' Isobel wrote in her diary that night. 'And I feel so confused. I've longed to be back, and now I'm here I don't feel at home. How stupid of me to think our house would be just as we left it. Of course the refugees from Paoshan changed things. They had to. When will I learn that it's never the same when you go back to a place.'

'I don't understand what's happening,' she confided in her husband. 'God has given me such a mother's heart, and everything I love seems to be taken away from me. You and I are separated so often and for so long. Our dear girlie's stuck in a Japanese internment camp. Homay has died and Lucius moved over the river.'

'You have Eva,' John pointed out.

'But... but I'm holding back from becoming too close to her, just in case she's taken away too.'

'When God takes away props, it's to force his people to lean more and more on him.'

'I know that,' his wife replied. 'But knowing it in my head is different from feeling it in my heart.'

And Danny Makes Four

Some of the Lisu Christians were deep in conversaton. 'I feel so jittery with all these soldiers in the area,' Sister Three said.

Her brother nodded. 'The missionaries don't seem to feel threatened. They go on as though nothing unusual is happening.'

Sister Three thought about that. 'I suppose they know better than we do. They get letters from everywhere. And their letters will be more reliable than our wind-words (worrying gossip).'

'Yes, I'm going to stop worrying about the soldiers and I'll tell the family to do the same.'

'I wish I could stop worrying just by telling myself to stop,' Sister Three thought.

For the next two years Isobel and John tried to continue 'as usual' but it was not always easy.

'Soldiers in strange uniforms are coming!' a Lisu boy called, running down the mountain trail into the village. People gathered all around him.

'How many?'

'Lots. Maybe a hundred!'

'Are they Japanese?'

'I don't know. They weren't wearing Japanese uniforms.'

'What should we do?'

'I think we should hide until they pass by.'

Isobel watched in amazement as a villageful of Lisu men, women, boys and girls, shimmied up mountain paths, down crevasses and behind rocks.

'They are like mountain goats,' she thought. 'Within minutes of the alarm, there's not a soul to be seen.'

Going into her home, Isobel prayed. 'Lord, whoever the soldiers are, please let them pass by the village. Please keep our people safe. And Lord, I pray for the Rainy Season Bible School students out on their weekend preaching assignments, please keep them safe from attack too.'

As the day passed, villagers trickled back home, none of them any the worse for their experience.

'Ma-Ma,' Eva said, the next morning, 'The RSBS students are coming. I can see a string of them on the mountainside across the valley.'

'Thank you, God,' Isobel prayed. 'Thank you.' And her heart sang.

Some of the villagers went out to meet the students.

'You were lucky you weren't here yesterday,' they told the returning band. 'A whole army of soldiers came past, soldiers dressed in a uniform we've never seen before.'

'They were Chinese,' a young man replied, 'but we don't know what their plans are.'

Then the time for the Girls' Bible School drew near again.

'Daddy is off on high adventure,' Isobel wrote to her daughter. 'He's trying to rescue Mr. and Mrs. Fred Hatton. They are at Stockade Hill which is still behind Japanese lines. I'm here with Charles Peterson. He and I work together here while Daddy is away on his trips. Preparing for the Girls' Bible School is keeping me very busy just now. The only thing is that we don't know if anyone will come. Many of the girls are afraid that if they leave their villages to come to Oak Flat and the Japanese invade their home villages while they are here they will never be able to get back to their families again!'

There was good news in Isobel's next weekly letter. 'Sweetheart Kathryn, I can't wait to tell you what has happened. After I wrote last week snow clouds came down over the highest mountains, and the wind blew icy cold. Lower down the snow turned to rain. The Salween girls have over twenty miles to travel, including crossing a dangerous river. I was sure they'd not do that in a snowstorm. By Saturday night we had over a dozen girls, all from the east bank. But all our best students are on the west side of the river. You can imagine how we prayed. Sunday continued stormy. But on Monday there was a lull. It didn't clear, but at least there were no downpours. Would the girls come? I wondered. (And I prayed too!).

You can imagine our thrill at sunset when a shout came ringing along the trail, "Girls from the west bank are coming!" We ran to the door, and around the edge of the mountain was a line of little dots moving down the trail toward us! We squelched out to meet them. There they were - their bedding and books in big bags slung over their shoulders or carried on their backs with the straps laced over their foreheads to distribute the weight. What chatter there was, darling Kathryn, as bare feet pattered over the muddy trails to the church kitchen where a warm fire and a hot supper were waiting.'

'Charles,' Isobel said, after evening worship with the girls. 'How awful it would have been if we'd cancelled the Girls' Bible School just because of the war going on around us.'

'Yes,' he agreed. 'They are splendid students, so keen to know God's Word and to tell other people about Jesus.'

'But I've noticed something quite different,' Eva said. She had helped to teach the classes. 'And it's not really to do with the girls.' Isobel and Charles looked puzzled. 'It seems to me that everyone in the village is much calmer, not so edgy about the war, and not so suspicious about strangers. I think that's because we've just gone on working as usual, and they assume from that that we think everything is all right.'

Charles Peterson stroked his chin thoughtfully. 'Eva, you may be right. I believe you're quite right!' There was a pause. 'And I think we should take the success with the girls as the Lord's guidance that we should go ahead with the short Bible School for teenage boys on 6th March, regardless of the current wind-words about gloom and disaster.'

Both women agreed.

The date in the diary was the 4th of March. A young man came rushing through the village to Isobel's house. 'Ma-Ma the postmaster at the town of Six Treasuries has run away. He's in hiding because he fears the arrival of the Japanese. They might come here too! Six Treasuries is just one day's journey away! Chinese soldiers are posted at the two ferry crossings, waiting to destroy the ferries if the Japanese get on them.'

Charles Peterson looked at Isobel. 'But if our boys come over on the ferries, then the boats are destroyed, they won't be able to get home at the end of the week!'

'Ma-Ma!' It was Eva. 'The cook says he must leave. His wife is homesick for her own people and he says he must take her there and settle in her village.'

'And it's pouring,' added Isobel, as though that was the very last thing they needed.

Looking at the women's faces, Charles took action. 'Let's get out of the rain, and let's pray.'

Hearts were poured out to the Lord as all three knelt on the floor. The rain was so heavy they couldn't hear each other's words, but God heard every one.

'How many boys have you counted?' Eva asked, beginning to doubt her own arithmetic.

Isobel smiled. 'Thirty-six. I've counted twice. It's the noise that makes it seem like twice that.'

'Well, you're not quite right,' Charles said.

'What do you mean?'

Charles smiled. 'Mr Yang, the principal of the church school, has decided to cancel all classes so that his students can attend too. By my reckoning that brings our numbers up to seventy-six.'

'But we have no cook!' wailed Eva.

She looked from Isobel to Charles and back to Isobel. 'There are some things men don't understand!' she announced. But God did. Seventy-six boys between the ages of ten and twenty attended the school. None went hungry, and they had their souls filled with God's Word.

Isobel often looked at the young boys and girls in Oak Flat and thought of little Kathryn. It was so long since she'd seen her daughter, she could hardly think what she would look like, now a teenager.

'Are you thinking about Kathryn?' John asked.

Isobel nodded. 'I'm just so glad that she was able to get a ship back to the States. Her foster family, the Sutherlands love her so much. She couldn't possibly have better foster parents. But how I long to see her, especially now.'

John looked down at his wife's ever increasing bump and fully understood. On August 1st 1943, Daniel Kuhn was born.

'How snow-white he is,' the village women said, when they came to see the new baby. 'And his hair is the colour of the sunrise.'

Isobel looked deep into her new son's eyes, dark pools that would one day be stirred by colour and beauty.

'Danny,' she whispered into his little shell ear, 'let me tell you about Kathryn. She's your big sister, and she's far, far away. One day you'll meet her and she'll love you to bits.'

Tears ran down John's face at the beauty of what he was seeing, mother and son falling deeply in love. Isobel looked up. Their eyes met. And in that instant John knew that he would always remember these precious moments of togetherness.

Danny was a hungry boy, too hungry to be satisfied by his mother's milk alone. Isobel recorded in her diary how they coped with that little problem. 'We got a herd of nanny goats and two billies. The older billy goat we've called Hitler. He likes to think he's boss and he has a passion for destruction!'

Then a call rang out.

'Ma-Ma! Hitler go storeroom! Make awful mess!' When Eva got excited she forgot most of her English. 'I go fix!'

Isobel got up and went out to see what was happening. Hitler was running for his life up the hill towards the refuge of his pen. Chasing him was a blur of blue Chinese gown from which a stick whacked out, sometimes striking Hitler, sometimes missing. 'Hitler might think he's a big goat he-man,' she said to John, who had just appeared to see the last of the spectacle, 'but when it's Hitler versus Eva, Hitler doesn't stand a chance!'

'Dear Daddy and Mummy, I just can't believe I have a baby brother! He sounds SO cute! I asked Uncle and Auntie Sutherland if they could send me airmail to Oak Flat so that I could see him, and check he has ten fingers and ten toes - did you do that, by the way? They said they thought that CIM might not be able to afford the mail charge! But it won't be long until we meet again, just a few months now. When I think about that I want to laugh and cry, but mostly laugh. Me a big sister. WOW!!!!

God bless you dearest Daddy and Mummy, and give a HUGE hug to Danny - but don't hurt him!

Much love Big Sister Kathryn

Ps. Don't let Danny grow until I've seen him. I want to see my baby brother when he's titchy!'

It was nearing time for the Kuhns to go home on furlough, and once again they were taking a new little Kuhn to meet the family in Canada and America. But apart from that things were very different from last time. Kathryn, who had finished at Chefoo, was now back in America at secondary school. She had had to travel back to America without ever seeing her parents. Isobel was always thankful for the loving care Kathryn received with her foster family, the Sutherlands. But now it was time for the Kuhns to be reuinited once more. On the last journey back to America Kathryn had travelled with her parents, this time she was waiting to welcome them home, waiting to see her little brother for the very first time.

As she prepared to leave Isobel thought over the work done in Lisuland. It was a way of counting her blessings and seeing what God had done.

'In 1942,' she wrote in her diary, 'we began a Bible School for girls. The following year was our first one for boys. In 1943 and 44 we started children's work. Eva was the stimulus, although I'd had it in mind for a long time. As soon as she could speak a bit of Lisu, she gathered the children of Oak Flat village together for a Bible Club every day or evening. We encouraged the girls from the Girls' Bible School to do the same when they went back to their own villages. What a way to spread the Gospel!'

'Allo Kafin'

'Say "bye bye" to Lisuland,' Isobel said, holding Danny up where the Oak Flat villagers could see him.

The one-year-old waved both hands in the air and gurgled his goodbyes. It was much easier for him to leave than for anyone else, as he had not yet learned the hurt of farewell. John hoisted his wife and child on to the truck and they rattled out of the village on the first leg of their very long journey to America ... and to Kathryn.

'Time for your lesson, Danny,' Isobel smiled. The boy beamed in response. 'Say Kathryn ... say Kathryn'

'Kafin,' he sprayed out, and laughed.

'Good boy! Now try again. Say Kathryn ... Kathryn.'

Danny decided this was a good game.

'Kafin,' he giggled at his cleverness. 'Kafin!'

The effort was worth his while. Isobel hugged him close.

'You'll have him giving a "Greetings to my Big Sister" speech by the time we see Kathryn,' John teased, as they clattered and rattled along the road.

'Look!' John said excitedly, not long after their plane took off for Calcutta. 'We're right over Lisuland.'

Struggling to unwind herself from Danny's grasp,

Isobel strained to look out of the window and catch a last glimpse of the country she loved so much. It was only Danny's repetition of 'Kafin', with its reminder that she was travelling ever nearer her daughter, that prevented tears from falling.

It was October 1944, and World War 2 was still being fought. Because of the war no passenger ships sailed from the Indian subcontinent to America. People wanting to return to their homeland had to take whatever transport was available. Bundled together as refugees, more often than not they found themselves crowded on board troopships.

'This heat!' Isobel exclaimed, tipping back Danny's sunhat to mop the perspiration off his forehead yet again.

'Oh for the ice-topped mountains of Lisuland,' sighed John. 'When it's cold you can always wrap up and get warm. But in this heat there is no way of cooling down.'

'I suppose we would get used to it if the Lord called us to work here.'

John Kuhn laughed. 'I hope that we're not going to be that long before transport is found for us!'

Some days after landing in Calcutta, they were transported to Bombay, there to await a troopship which they had been told was going to America.

'Why won't they tell us what route we're going to take?' Isobel asked her husband.

He looked serious. 'Belle, the war we've lived through for the last few years is nothing to what we're going to meet now. We're not told our route or our destination, and quite right too. Passengers would be in real danger if the facts got out, they could be subject to kidnapping or worse, and if they were taken and tortured until they divulged their route, a whole shipful of troops and passengers could find itself torpedoed and at the bottom of the ocean.'

Isobel shivered despite the heat. Travelling in wartime was not comfortable. John Kuhn was in the hold with the other male civilians, and allowed to see his wife and child for just two hours each day. Isobel and Danny shared an officer's cabin with nine other women and children. They slept in bunks three tiers high. Isobel's cabin was next to the ship's cinema, and the noise from the films blasted through the thin walls till nearly midnight.

'All women will report to the ship's officer for a lecture,' boomed the loudspeaker. Isobel was herded there with the others. Clearing his throat, the ship's officer pulled himself to his full height, then gave his charges to the women.

'It is my duty to inform you that you are on board this ship as an act of charity. This is not a passenger ship, and there is no accommodation on it for children. No baby food is carried therefore don't ask for it. No part of the ship is safe for babies and children, some decks have no railings, and hawse-holes are uncovered. If your child falls overboard, we will not stop to pick it up. It is up to each mother to watch her own children. There are no laundry facilities other than the wash-hand basins. You will eat at the officers' mess, and will finish your meal and clear up after it in the space of half-an-hour. Meals will be served promptly and you will queue beforehand. Are there any questions?'

But he left the platform without giving anyone the opportunity to respond, leaving behind him a room full of women who wondered how they were going to survive the next thirty-six days.

'Danny, my big boy!' John said, relieving his wife of their fifteen month old son. Isobel slid down to a sitting position on the lower deck of the ship. 'Are you all right?' her husband asked in a concerned voice.

Isobel's eyes drooped. 'I'm just exhausted. Utterly exhausted. Every waking minute of Danny's day, I have to carry him in case he slips. If he fell through a hawse-hole we'd never see him again.' She was near to tears. Danny struggled in his father's arms and reached for his mother.

'No, young man,' John said. 'For the two hours each day that I have the privilege of your company, you'll stay in my arms and let your poor mama have a rest.' Isobel smiled weakly. 'Let's see what we can do for Mum,' John said.

He took off his belt, tied one end of his handkerchief through the buckle and tied the other end of the hankie round Danny's wrist. Then, kneeling down beside his wife, he put the other end of his belt under his knee, so confining Danny to within the belt's length of himself. The toddler sat down in disgust. Ignoring the fit of pique,

John massaged Isobel's shoulders, back and upper arms, eventually feeling them relax and unwind. Soon Isobel had had enough - she was asleep.

But John was only free to help for two hours a day. The other twenty-two felt like forever. Especially traumatic was the long wait in the meal queues three times each day.

'Lord,' Isobel cried out silently from under Danny's weight in the queue one day. Her head swam. Was she going to faint?

'Well, now, look at our poor mother carrying this big heavy boy and me doing nothing!' Two strong arms removed Danny. God had heard her cry and answered with another missionary also travelling home.

'Mother,' the friendly missionary said, 'from now on I'm Danny's nurse. Before every meal I'll come and get him, wash him and carry him in. After we've eaten I'll bring him out. Do you hear?'

Isobel hardly heard, so great were the songs of praise that were rising from her head, her heart, her weary arms and her leaden legs! And the missionary kept her word.

After thirty-six days at sea, the ship approached the coast of America. But which coast?

'What will happen when we land?' Isobel asked a friend and fellow missionary. 'If we don't know which port we're going into, how can we get someone to meet us?

'The Lord will have something waiting for us,' was the reply. 'He hasn't brought us all this way to desert us now.'

The boat berthed, and John, Isobel and Danny spent their first few minutes on American soil without the first clue where they were. But, by nightfall, having landed at 10am, they were in the Los Angeles office of the China Inland Mission.

Their daughter, Kathryn, was several days' travelling away, and Danny cried most of the time.

'Mr Sutherland had thoughtfully arranged for us to meet Kathryn alone in a little room,' Isobel confided in her diary. 'Our little girlie, whom we had last seen at seven-and-a-half years of age, was now thirteen, and almost grown up. We had tried to get to her once in those years, but the Japanese bombed a bridge on our only road and we had to turn back. At today's reunion the Lord melted us all together into one. There was no feeling of strangeness. Praise his name!'

'Allo Kafin,' Danny said, tentatively at first, then with greater enthusiasm. 'Kafin! Kafin!'

Kathryn held her arms out to her little brother. He looked at his father, then at his mother. Both smiled. Danny then toddled to his sister, raised his arms to be lifted, and hugged her. 'Allo Kafin,' he said, snuggling into her neck, and planting a kiss somewhere in the region of her ear. Tears flowed down the girl's face. 'I'm so happy,' she sobbed into Danny's sun-gold hair. 'I'm just so happy.'

John and Isobel watched as their children fell in love with each other.

The next six months, which should have been a relaxing time, was rather fraught. Like many missionaries on home leave, the Kuhns were house guests with family members. Danny was a normal toddler who got into absolutely everything. And Isobel was a normal mother. She nearly tore her hair out!

'If you feel it's the Lord's will for you to do a course at Dallas Theological Seminary, then he will provide the means and a home for us,' Isobel reassured her husband.

'I know that,' he said. 'And I'm looking forward to seeing how he does it.'

John was wide-eyed and open-mouthed when he read his mail a few days later. 'Belle,' he said. 'The $2000 worth of shares Father left me ten years ago are now worth $6000!' He sat down. 'That means we can look for a place in Dallas.'

Isobel smiled. 'God knows our needs. I couldn't cope much longer here. We need to be on our own.'

'I understand,' her husband agreed. 'As a family of four we've hardly spent a night on our own.'

Isobel had recovered herself. 'Let's work out what to pray for.' Within ten minutes they were both on their knees with their list before them.

1. Our house must cost less than $5000 - this leaves $1000 for furnishings etc.

2. We must have access by 28th July.

3. Since we have no car, can the house be near enough to the seminary so that John can walk there?

4. And it should be near to the High School so that Kathryn can walk.

5. It should have two bedrooms.

6. It should have a fenced-in back garden for Danny to play in safely.

The Kuhns wrote to all the property agents in Dallas, but only one held out any hope of finding such a property. It was agreed that Isobel should go to Dallas for a month to find a home for them, and to have a break. Kathryn, who was just beginning her school summer holidays, was delighted to look after her little brother.

'Don't you know what the war has done to the housing market?' Isobel was asked over and over again when she arrived in Dallas. 'There's hardly a house for sale, let alone at your price. Most are sold before they ever reach our books.'

Taking no notice of the prophets of doom, Isobel went to the one estate agent who had held out hope to them, and requested an interview.

'There's just the place we told you about, Mrs. Kuhn,' the office manager said. 'And it's ages since a similar place came on the market - though this isn't actually on the market yet. It's a five roomed cottage, with a fenced-in back garden, and it's within walking distance of both the school and the seminary. I think you could get it for $4500. The one snag is that the owner doesn't want to move by 28th July as he won't have entry to his new premises by then. However, I'll take you to meet him.'

The words spun in Isobel's head. God seemed to be answering their prayer in every detail except one, but it was an important one.

'The owners are Christians,' she told John on the phone that evening, 'and so easy to talk to. I explained that if we couldn't get possession on time, there was no point in us pursuing it. And, guess what?'

John couldn't guess.

'They've agreed to let us have it on 28th July, and they'll stay with their daughter for a month before moving into their new home!'

'Praise the Lord!' John nearly shouted.

And Isobel joined in.

When John arrived in Dallas with Kathryn and Danny, Isobel was restored and refreshed, and the house was home. For the year that followed the Kuhns lived a normal family life, and how they enjoyed it. But it seemed no time at all till their time together drew to its end and John left for China.

High Drama

'Don't cry. Promise you won't cry Kathryn!' three-year-old Danny called to his sister, as their train drew out of Philadelphia. Isobel's vision blurred with tears as she waved to her daughter and the Sutherlands, into whose foster care Kathryn was again committed.

'Bye Danny,' his sister called. 'Byeeee.'

When she thought she could no longer be seen, Kathryn turned to her loving foster mother, and wept as though she would never stop.

'You promise me not to cry too,' Danny said, looking up into his mother's face.

Isobel sat down, pulled Danny on to her knee, and faced him out the window. Tears swelled from her eyes and ran down her face, one trickling down Danny's neck. He scratched at the tear thinking it was an itch.

'What a difference this is from our passage home,' Isobel told her fellow passengers.

'It certainly is,' agreed one of the women, having heard Isobel's story. 'You've exchanged a troopship for a cargo vessel, and hundreds of fellow passengers for a few excellent travelling companions, as well as the crew, of course.'

'But there are still no railings,' Isobel said, grabbing for Danny who was venturing too near the edge of the deck for safety.

Entertaining the children was difficult and it seemed that they had an insatiable appetite for storys. "Do you want a story?" The answer was always 'yes'. And they said 'yes' to the idea of a Sunday School too. By the time the voyage was well underway, the children had requested a Sunday School every day of the week!

After forty-six days at sea on a cargo boat, Isobel and Danny disembarked at Shanghai wharf, expecting John to be there to meet them. He was not.

'Things are so difficult here since the war,' they were told at the CIM office. 'Bridges the Japanese blew up are still not repaired, and transport to the far interior is nearly, but not quite, impossible. Your husband will be here just as soon as he can be.'

Isobel had plenty of time to wonder how she and Danny would get back to Lisuland, but John when he came, solved the problem.

'You will have to go by air to Yunnan Province, and I'll go with the men by truck. We'll take the luggage with us.'

'Am I really going in an aeroplane?' Danny asked, in great excitement. Isobel told him he was.

'What kind is it?'

'An army freighter. It's called a Flying Fortress.'

'Will it take as long as the ship did?' wondered Danny. John hugged him. 'I don't think so!' he laughed. 'You leave one morning and arrive that afternoon.'

'I wish Kathryn was here,' he said, disappointed. 'She'd like going on a Flying Fortress too.'

The thought tugged at his mum's heart-strings.

After some time in Paoshan setting up a mission house there, Isobel and Danny set out for Lisuland, three months ahead of John, who had other work to do first. Lucius, who had spent nearly a year away from home, travelled back with them. Chinese coolies carried their luggage.

'What's happened to all the villages?' Isobel asked, puzzled by the abandoned homes they passed along the way.

'There are so many bandits,' her companion explained, 'people don't feel safe any longer living in remote places.'

Sadness filled Isobel's heart as they journeyed through deserted village after deserted village.

'Is Oak Flat like this?' she asked eventually.

'No Ma-Ma, it's not like this. It's not as you left it, but the people are still there. That's what Mary told me in her letters.'

Whatever the changes were in Oak Flat village, the welcome the Kuhns received was heartwarming. Isobel wrote to John, 'At the last steep 2000 foot climb, Lisu with horses were waiting for us. Oh, what a loving jubilant reunion! Danny had a horse to himself, and two Lisu, one on each side, walked close beside to guard him. "Mummy! My horse has bells and yours doesn't!" he shouted. "My horse rides bumpily." At the end of the climb a delicious feast of pork was given to us. What a welcome party.'

'Is this our home?' Danny asked, when everyone melted into the quickly setting sun.

Isobel looked around her. 'Yes,' she said with a quiver in her voice, 'We're home.'

'Please don't let our house fall over into the canyon,' the little boy prayed before curling up on his rough wooden bed.

And Isobel knew why. The shanty, which was twelve years old, tilted precariously towards the edge of the precipice. Great chunks of thatch were missing and the dust of nine months lay over everything.

'Some of the Christians seem as covered in dust as the house was when we arrived back,' Isobel told Lucius, when he visited Oak Flat to make arrangements for the 1947 Rainy Season Bible School.

'The war has affected people in many ways,' the young man explained. 'Some of the Christians looked for protection to Lisuland owners, but after a while they forget that God is their Protector.' He paused. 'And some we thought were believers have fallen away altogether.'

John's return, just before the School was due to begin, encouraged them all.

'We have a record number of students this year,' John announced, looking up from the list of those who had said they were coming. 'How will we accommodate them all?'

'I could teach my evangelism classes in the Chinese

schoolhouse,' Isobel suggested. 'That would ease the strain.'

'What a good idea!'

'We've a lot to thank Eva for,' Isobel went on. 'The children's work was her brainchild. Lucius got the idea for his Sunday School from her class here in Oak Flat.'

'I remember,' John nodded. 'And how God has used them. Think of it. If all our RSBS students carried the vision of a Sunday School class back to their own villages, a whole generation of Lisu children would hear the gospel, and from their own people. That's the ideal,' he added. 'Missionaries should always be trying to work themselves out of their jobs. But that time hasn't come yet.'

Soon after the Bible School ended, John was off again on his travels.

1947 and 1948 produced troubles Isobel could well have done without, especially as John was often away and her nearest missionary neighbour was many days' journey away. News came to Isobel about their Lisu friends, Keh-deh-seh-pa and Pade-John who were no longer living a Christian life.

'I find it so hard to believe what's happening,' she told one of the Lisu elders. 'Keh-deh-seh-pa seemed one of our keenest men. It was he who gave us the land for the church. It breaks my heart to think that he's fallen into such sin that he's had to be put out of his office as a church deacon. And it's awful to hear that Pade-John is going down the same road.'

Isobel wondered how the situation could possibly be any worse than it was. She could not have begun to imagine what would happen within the year. Dark secrets were hidden in her diary.

'Keh-deh-seh-pa and his son came to the house last night to threaten me. Thank God, a poor Christian farmer saw them sneaking round the house and followed them in, pretending he wanted to sell me some charcoal!'

'Our water supply has been taken away from us. I'm being persecuted, and by people who would claim to be Christians. Help me to love them, Lord.'

'Our goat-herd had an accident. I can't work out exactly what happened. No one will tell me. Very suspicious.'

Just as things were getting dangerous, Charles Peterson arrived back from home leave, and was followed soon afterwards by John, just in time for the 1948 Rainy Season Bible School.

'How good God is,' Isobel almost sang. 'There is even a group of students from Burma.'

But the school, which was a splendid success, ended with high drama.

'What on earth are Keh-deh-seh-pa and Pade-John up to?' John asked, as the two men led a rabble of farmers up the hill towards the RSBS. 'They're all armed with clubs!'

'Not all,' observed Isobel. 'Keh-deh-seh-pa's wife and the young man she's too friendly with are in the midst of them, trussed like hens.'

'Ruth and Jana? What are they going to do with them?'

The former deacon strode up to the missionaries. 'They have sinned and now they're to be beaten.'

Isobel called to one of the Lisu Christian women 'Take Danny where he can't see or hear what's happening.'

The little boy was escorted up the mountain trail.

'Don't go into the kitchen,' a student told Isobel, when she had seen her son safely off. 'The mob has tied Ruth to one wall and Jana to the other. Keh-deh-seh-pa has tried them under Chinese law. He says they've sinned and will remain tied until Ma-Pa signs a paper saying Pade-John can be the mid-Salween pastor!'

Isobel's mouth hung open in astonishment.

'Don't be hasty,' the student said, as she was about to storm into the kitchen, 'remember they are working under Chinese law and this is China.'

Isobel stopped in her tracks. She couldn't do a thing.

'Ma-Ma!' Danny's shrill voice cut through the tense air. 'I'm home and I'm hungry.'

So were all the RSBS students. In the absence of an alternative, Isobel prepared the meal with a prisoner tied on either side of her. Keh-deh-seh-pa and John were locked in discussion.

'Go to bed,' John told her, after darkness fell. 'We could be here for hours yet.'

Isobel lay in bed fully clothed and prayed. Suddenly the air filled with shouting.

'May I come in, Ma-Ma?' Lucius' voice asked.

'What's happened?' she exclaimed.

The young man's voice shook as he spoke.

'An old man from church went to cut the prisoners free. But Keh-deh-seh-pa's crowd heard of it and stormed up the hill, caught him and were just about to club him when Mr Kuhn called out that he would sign the paper. Then they let him go.'

'But he didn't sign, did he?!'

'The paper is not worth anything. The old man's life is worth more,' comforted Lucius.

'You've told her?' It was John. He was standing just inside the door.

The following morning the students got up early and left for their villages well before daybreak. When the Kuhns arose, they found a letter had been slipped under their door. It was from the mid-Salween students. John read it aloud.

'Dear Pastor Kuhn. We are leaving before dawn so that Pade-John will not see us go. We hear that he planned to go back with us. We don't want such a man for our pastor! We know you were forced to sign the paper, but we are hurrying back to warn the mid-Salween church that it was forced from you. We won't have him.'

'Dear good people,' Isobel breathed. 'They understand.'

'You'll have to move to my village,' Lucius insisted that morning. 'Ma-Pa, when you are away it is no longer safe for Ma-Ma and Danny to remain here.'

In December 1948, the Kuhns and Charles Peterson moved to Olives village. But Isobel left a little bit of her heart behind, so much did she love the Oak Flat people.

Then some time later there was a visitor to Olives - Keh-deh-seh-pa came looking for forgiveness.

Four months after the missionaries left Oak Flat, it was overrun and ravaged by Communist outlaws. God had moved his servants to safety just in time.

All Change

Isobel Kuhn's days working among her beloved Lisu people were numbered.

'What does this word mean?' six-year-old Danny asked innocently. He mentioned a word which made Isobel catch a breath. She tried to hide her shock. Sitting on the ground outside the shack that was to be her last home in Lisuland, she gathered Danny on to her knee.

'There are some words,' she explained, 'that God's people should never say. These words make God sad.'

Danny looked stricken. 'I didn't want to make God sad,' he said, his eyes filling with tears.

Isobel hugged him close. 'I know that,' she assured him, planting a kiss on his cheek. 'You're too young to know good words from bad when you hear them.'

'But I do know some bad words,' Danny said defiantly, 'but I don't say them ... not if I know they're bad. But I didn't know what that word meant.'

That night Isobel prayed for her son. 'How much longer,' she asked God, 'can Danny be kept in this village where most people aren't Christians, and where their lives are no example for my, ever watchful, Danny?'

In her heart of hearts Isobel knew that her time in Lisuland was coming to an end.

On 10th March 1950, after a time of real danger and personal threat, John Kuhn stood on an outcrop of rock, and waved a heart-rending goodbye to his wife and son as they set out for Burma and safety. Snowy mountain passes, bad tempered border guards, frustrating delays, officious soldiers and government red tape all had to be got through before the pair of them boarded a ship for Canada.

Arriving at Vancouver, the port from which she had sailed to China nearly twenty-two years previously, Isobel found herself wrapped in the love of old friends. But, comfortable and comforting though that was, she wasted no time at all in making her way south to America, to Wheaton in Illinois, where her daughter Kathryn was at college.

'I just can't believe we're together,' Kathryn said one evening, after they had worship together.

Danny made no comment. Both his mother and sister noticed his unaccustomed silence. Rising to their feet in unison, Isobel and Kathryn pulled the boy to his feet and held him in their nightly triangular hug.

'There's just one thing missing,' Danny said.

'What's that?' asked Kathryn, though she already knew the answer. Her brother thought for just a second before he answered. 'Whiskers.'

Isobel's heart lurched. She knew exactly what Danny meant, for she too missed John's rough whiskery hug.

But a whole year had to pass before John Kuhn left China, and some months more before the nightly cuddle was a foursome and whiskery. After such a long absence there was the past to talk about and the future to discuss.

'But I'm fifty!' Isobel protested, when her husband first suggested working in Thailand. 'I'm too old.'

John stretched out in his chair. Clasping his hands behind his head he looked long and hard at his wife. 'We are neither of us young,' he said. 'But there are 5000 Lisu people in North Thailand, 5000 souls who need to hear about Jesus.'

Isobel's heart strings tugged, but her mind threw up all kinds of objections. 'I'm too old to learn another language,' she announced firmly. 'My brain wouldn't cope.'

'Objection one overruled,' John smiled. 'We can use our Chinese. I've hardly been anywhere in North Thailand where my Chinese wasn't understood by someone.'

'Chinese!' Isobel gulped. 'My Chinese is as rusty as a stable door hinge! I tell you, my mind is beyond that.'

'Objection two overruled. You said you couldn't learn a new language. Brushing up an old one is not the same thing.'

'But they need young people,' she argued, 'with energy. Think of the steepness of the mountain trails!'

'Bang goes objection three. Your experience makes up for anything you lack in energy.'

'Who's to say we could get in?' Isobel asked.

John grinned. 'That's my girl!'

Isobel knew what she'd known all along; if God wanted the Kuhns in Thailand, they would go to Thailand.

That battle won, Isobel prepared to fight another. Going to Thailand meant leaving, Kathryn and Danny behind. Friends, who had nine children of their own, welcomed him and he was soon comfortably lost in the happy little crowd. Kathryn then enrolled in a Bible College and Isobel, despite all her protestations, found herself learning the rudiments of the Thai language.

'How are you doing?' John asked, seeing her brow crumpled in concentration.

'It's only the thought of those 5000 Lisu that keeps me going,' his wife replied wearily. 'And they'll never know what it cost me to learn their language.'

'And we'll never know what it cost Jesus to save us,' said John.

Immediately Isobel's brow unfurrowed, her back straightened, and she picked up the Thai book determinedly. 'You're right.' Her voice was brighter than it had been all evening. 'This is a small price to pay.'

And it was with that thought in both their minds that the Kuhns left Kathryn and Danny behind, and travelled the long, long way to Thailand.

Yellow robed Buddhist priests seemed to throng Bangkok, at least that was what it felt like to Isobel.

'Some are just boys,' she pointed out to her husband.

He nodded. 'Their families think they'll get credit in the next life if they send their sons to be priests for a year or two.'

The sadness of it all hit her. Some of the boys were no older than Danny. 'What a hopeless situation,' she thought, 'always struggling and never winning, as if any one of us could ever gain enough credits to go to heaven.'

The temples and priests felt oppressive and Isobel was not sorry to leave Bangkok behind, to climb aboard the train for Chiengmai in northern Thailand. But she could not leave Buddhism behind. Temples peppered the landscape through which they travelled.

No sooner did they arrive in Chiengmai than John's work as mission superintendent took up all his time. But Isobel had her hands full too. The mission at Chiengmai was like the hub of a wheel. Mail for all the missionaries in the area arrived there to be sorted and sent on, with encouraging little notes added before directing them on their way.

'You've no idea how much your letters mean to us,' a visiting missionary told her one day. 'Being so far from home makes the mission family especially precious.'

'I discovered that for myself when we were separated for long years from Kathryn,' Isobel told her guest. 'No other letters made up for the ones we didn't get from our darling daughter, but they were a comfort.'

While John was often away, much of Isboel's time was spent at base, but her work was very varied. Isobel Kuhn wiped tears from sad faces and held close those whose hearts were aching and broken. She discussed projects and prayed with those involved in them. When new workers arrived, she found language teachers for them, then helped with their stumbling grammar, adding new words in each conversation to increase their vocabularies. When relationship problems arose, and they did with missionaries as they do with everyone else, Isobel was wise with her advice and faithful with her prayers for those who were going through troubled times. Many missionaries and national Christians thanked God that the Kuhns had gone to Thailand.

'I don't understand it,' Isobel told John one day. 'My experience is working with tribal people, living in shanty huts on my own or with one or two others, growing vegetables for the table and cooking little meals for ourselves.' Her husband knew what was coming. 'Now, here I am running a guest-house, organising massive shopping and overseeing the cooking of vast quantities of food. But do you know what puzzles me most?'

John waited to find that out.

'I feel I don't have many opportunities to speak to people about the Lord Jesus, at least, not to people who don't already know him.'

They prayed about that.

'Are you sure it's all right for me to stay, Mrs. Kuhn?' a young American asked not long afterwards. Isobel opened her home and her heart. 'You see,' the girl explained, 'I'm not a Christian. I don't believe in it at all. I'm more interested in eastern religions. I want to find out more about them while I'm here. That's an advantage of travelling around the world, you can find out what all sorts of people believe then make up your own mind.'

Her hostess wisely did not jump in with a sermon. The woman and the girl talked into the evening, until

Isobel excused herself, saying that she had to be up early in the morning.

'Why's that?' the visitor asked.

Isobel smiled. 'I meet with my best friend at 5.30 every morning.'

The girl's eyebrows rose dramatically. 'You meet someone at 5.30! People keep early hours in these parts!'

'The friend I meet neither slumbers nor sleeps,' Isobel explained. 'He watches over me day and night, so 5.30am is not a problem for him.'

'You mean God?'

Isobel Kuhn nodded. A puzzled young face looked up. 'I've never heard anyone call God a friend before.'

Isobel sat down again, late though it was. 'He's been my friend for more years than you've lived,' she explained to her guest. 'And I want to tell you just one thing before I go off to bed. You'll not find a follower of any eastern religion who can call his god his friend.'

Leaving the girl to think that through, Isobel took herself to her bedroom, her heart rejoicing as she went. I'm still a missionary, she thought delightedly, God still has people he wants me to talk to. The following morning she spent time with, God, her Heavenly Friend, before making breakfast for her guest. A lot of serious talking was done that day.

'And I thought I'd become a hotelier,' Isobel Kuhn sighed as she heaved herself over a rock on the rough track that was pleased to call itself a road.

John laughed. 'Let's rest a while,' he suggested.

The pair of them sat on the shady side of the rock over which they had scrambled, and relaxed.

'I love the smell of the wet earth,' Isobel said. 'During the year I spent in Wheaton with Kathryn and Danny I used to walk through the park, but there was none of the earthy smell we have here.'

'I know what you mean. Back home nature has been so well organised, there's hardly anything of its wildness left. But if the gardeners who plant regimented lines of flowers could only see how they grow here in the wild, they'd never plant another straight row again!'

His wife grinned. 'You're right.'

John hoisted himself to his feet and, taking his wife by the hand, pulled her up to join him.

'There's work to be done,' he said. 'And we want to arrive before dark.'

'Ma-Ma's coming!' a girl in the mountain village called out, just as the sun set. 'I can hear her voice.'

The little girl's father and mother stopped what they were doing. In the distance, but ringing clearly through the still air, they could hear the sound of singing, joyful, heart-felt singing.

'No-one sings like Ma-Ma,' her mother said. 'It's as though her heart overflows and all the sweetness pours out in the words of her song. Just listen.'

'Heaven above is softer blue,

Earth around is sweeter green;

Something lives in every hue,

Christless eyes have never seen:

Birds with gladder songs o'erflow,
Flowers with deeper beauties shine,
Since I know, as now I know,
I am his, and he is mine.'

'What do the words mean?' the girl asked.

'You'll have to ask Ma-Ma,' her father told her. 'She'll translate them for you. She speaks Thai well. Now,' he said, 'run round the village and tell the Christians to come for a meeting.'

Isobel's voice grew louder as they neared the village and by the time they arrived, a welcome party awaited them.

'How did you know we were coming?' asked Isobel.

John laughed heartily.

That night, by the light of tiny oil lamps, the believers sang praises to God. Isobel translated the song she had sung, and everyone learned it. After teaching for several days the Kuhns moved to the next Christian community. The elder there wanted to know what was happening outside Thailand.

'Communism has completely overtaken China now,' John explained sadly.

'What will happen to the Christians there?' the old man asked.

Isobel prayed that John would be given the right words to explain the situation.

'God says that he will be with us always,' her husband said. 'That promise is to believers in Communist lands too.'

'Will they be able to meet as a church?'

'I doubt it. I very much doubt it.'

'Will they be allowed to preach the Gospel?'

'No. Not publicly.'

'And the missionaries...?'

Isobel's eyes filled with tears as her husband answered.

'All missionaries are out of China now. The people are on their own, but they are on their own with God.'

The grey head bent forward, and in a rush of Thai the old man poured out prayer for his brothers and sisters in Jesus who were condemned to live in a Communist state.

The trek home to Chiengmai was long, but the time was precious. So much of the Kuhns' married life had seen them in different places. In any case, it gave them time to talk.

'The little Chinese village churches seemed so weak,' Isobel said, as they discussed the onward march of Communism. 'Do you think they will survive?'

'I don't know whether they will survive as organised groups,' her husband answered, 'but the real believers are safe in the arms of Jesus. Whatever happens to them, when their time comes to go home, they will go home to heaven.'

There was a long silence before he made his final comment on the subject.

'But I fear many of them will reach heaven through violent deaths at the hands of the Communists.'

And in her heart, Isobel felt that was true.

Journey's End

'Watch your feet!' one of the company warned, as the little group of Christians climbed in single file up the mountain trail.

Everyone looked down as they walked, taking care not to turn their ankles on the stones, or slip in the mud between them. Suddenly the person in front of Isobel stood on the end of a fallen branch, misjudging its stability. The other end sprung in the air striking Isobel a glancing blow. The man in front swung round. 'Are you all right?' he asked, seeing the colour drain from her face.

The little group gathered round in concern.

'I'll be fine in a minute,' she said, though the pain was so severe that the world swam around her.

After a time, Isobel insisted that they continue the trek. She didn't realise that the group had slowed down considerably, so great was her struggle to cope with the pain.

On returning to the city she consulted a missionary doctor.

'I'm pretty sure the pain is coming from a torn ligament,' he assured her.

So, leaving the accident behind her, Isobel got on with the work she had to do.

Seven months later, she was again climbing another slippery slope to a tribal village. Her foot slid in the mud and Isobel crashed to the ground, landing on a jagged tree stump. Her companions rushed to help her up.

'Leave me for a minute,' she gasped, trying to get her breath back.

When she seemed a little better they helped her to her feet. But Isobel's legs gave way under her. Sitting her down on a smooth rock, they gathered around their friend and prayed that God would relieve her pain. She had a very uncomfortable trek down the hill, especially as she was injured in exactly the same place as before.

'It looks quite clear,' was the diagnosis, as the doctor held the X-ray up to the light of the window. 'There doesn't seem to be any damage done.'

Thanking God for caring for her once again, Isobel got up and got on.

'What a lot of energy you have!' a new missionary told her one day as they walked from one tribal village to another. 'I'm struggling to keep up with you!'

Isobel laughed, thinking that the young woman was just half her age. 'I've never felt better in my life,' she said. 'And I'm grateful for that. When John and I first talked about coming to Thailand, I argued that my mind was too old to learn another language, and that my body was too old to cope with mountain treks. Now here I am helping to teach you Thai and climbing up to the villages to introduce you to the work you'll be doing there. I've a lot to be grateful for.'

'What an amusing time I've had today,' she wrote to Danny that evening. 'When climbing up the hill with our new worker, I discovered that I have more stamina than she has - and she's nearer your age than mine! Then, when we arrived in the village and met with the believers for prayer, I was still wide awake and looking forward to their fellowship when I realised that at the Amen the young woman had not raised her head. She had fallen asleep during the prayers! One ancient villager noticed too. Turning to me she grinned from ear to ear. "It's the old ones like you and me that can keep going," she whispered. And she looked over eighty! Your Mama is having a crisis! What am I - a young agile goat who thrives on climbing mountains or an old one like my ancient friend?!'

'I think I should go to the doctor,' Isobel told John, about a year after her fall. 'I'm a bit concerned about the site of my injury.'

Her husband agreed, and arrangements were made for her visit.

On examining the area, this time the doctor looked serious. 'This needs further investigation,' he told his patient and friend. 'I want to refer you to a specialist in Bangkok.'

'I'll try to fit that in soon,' Isobel said thoughtfully.

The doctor sat down and looked at her. 'It needs seen to immediately,' he insisted. 'This could be very serious.'

Arrangements were made for an urgent trip to Bangkok, and the extended missionary family centred in

Chiengmai were much in prayer for their friend while she was away.

John's face broke into a wide grin and his eyes sparkled with tears, a mixture of joy and relief.

'The tests show that there is no malignancy?' he said, as if to reassure himself.

The missionary doctor nodded. 'That's what they say.'

And when the Kuhns arrived back at the mission house, nobody needed to ask the result. It was written all over their faces! Worship that evening was like a party in prayer, so happy were those who were there.

But, deep inside herself, Isobel was not convinced that all was well. And over the following few days, when thoughts of possible cancer bothered her, she reminded herself that even if she had cancer she was still safe in Jesus' care.

Having been in Bangkok, she was a little behind in her work, so the next week was a busy one, finishing on the Saturday with guests for a meal. But an unexpected visitor arrived just before the guests did. It was the missionary doctor.

John puzzled asked, 'What brings you here?'

The doctor sat down. The world seemed to stop. 'I've just heard from Bangkok,' he began, looking directly at Isobel. 'The news is not as good as we thought. It seems that there is cancer and that surgery is an absolute necessity.'

Isobel was silent.

'A surgeon from Bangkok is on his way. He's staying

in Chiengmai for just 48 hours. He'd like to operate tomorrow.'

'But I've got guests,' Isobel said without thinking.

That evening in the mission house was little different from usual. Isobel welcomed her visitors, saw to their needs, and made sure that an enjoyable evening was spent together.

The following morning, while her guests were still in bed, Isobel and John drove to the hospital and major surgery was done. As soon as she had recovered enough to travel, Isobel was flown out of Thailand and back to the United States. Once again she travelled alone, John remaining behind. As the plane took off she could hear his words in her head. 'If your treatment goes well I'll stay until we were due to go on home leave. That's just a year from now. But if it doesn't, I'll fly right out to be with you.'

And John, standing beside the tarmac at Bangkok airport, thought of the letter his wife had left at the mission house. Its closing words were etched into his heart. 'I thank the Lord for each one of you, and would leave you Philippians 3:13,14: "Brethren, this one thing I do, forgetting those things which are behind ... I press toward ... Christ Jesus." Let this be the ruling thing in your life as I wish it to be in mine.'

It was November 1954, almost exactly twenty-six years since Isobel had stepped off *The Empress of Russia* on to Chinese soil.

From the aloneness of her long flight home, the

returning missionary found herself surrounded by friends. But best of all there was Kathryn.

'My sweetheart,' Isobel said, holding her daughter as close as she could, her wound still being sore. 'My own dear Kathryn.'

And the hours they spent together that evening were precious.

'I heard just two days ago that I've been accepted for China Inland Mission,' Kathryn told her mother.

Isobel, lying in bed, was flooded with peace and joy.

'From time to time over the years I've wondered how all our separations would affect you and Danny,' Isobel told her daughter. 'We've not exactly had a normal family life. Your dad and I have spent so long apart, and most of your lives have not been with us. But the fact that you're answering God's call to work with CIM reassures me.'

Kathryn was silent as she tried to find words to express her thoughts.

'Sometimes it was really hard,' she admitted. 'When I was at Chefoo I wondered if I would ever see you and Dad again. Then when Danny was born, that was another difficult time. It was so strange knowing I had a baby brother and not being able to see him.' Then Kathryn laughed. 'But when we eventually met it was love at first sight.'

'But you are willing to follow in our footsteps, knowing what it might mean?'

'I'm willing,' said Kathryn. 'And CIM is willing to take me.'

'It's so hard to see Mum like this,' Kathryn Kuhn confided in a friend. 'The treatments are taking such a lot out of her. I'm not sure how she'll cope with Danny's visit at Christmas.'

'Does she know about it yet?'

'No, the person who is paying his plane fare wants it to be a surprise. We'll not spring it on her though, she's not well enough for that.'

'And your departure?' the girl asked tentatively.

'That's scheduled for 24th February.'

There was a lengthy silence.

'If it's God's will for me to go, then I'll go,' Kathryn said firmly. Her friend smiled.

'What's so funny?'

'You sound exactly like your mother!'

When Isobel heard about Danny's coming visit, she paced herself so that she would be able to cope with a lively eleven-year-old. And that's just what arrived off the coast-to-coast plane.

'I must be the happiest mother in America!' she told Kathryn and Danny. 'To have you both here for Christmas is more than I could have hoped for.'

Danny beamed. 'And I knew before you did that I was coming.'

Isobel agreed, 'You had the edge on me there.'

'But you knew before I did that Kathryn was going to be a missionary.'

'That's us quits then.'

Kathryn laughed at the pair of them.

'What will Dad be doing today?' Danny asked, as they ate their Christmas dinner.

'I think he might be celebrating Christmas at Chiengmai. It's such a busy place with people coming and going all the time that it often has a party atmosphere, whatever the time of year.'

Kathryn wondered where she would be next Christmas. Then a sad thought passed through her mind. 'Where will mum be? Will she still be alive?'

Isobel read the expression on her daughter's face.

'Wherever Dad is he'll be thinking about us, and he'll be thinking about the Lord Jesus Christ. And do you know something?' Kathryn and Danny looked at their mother. 'Only relatively few people saw Jesus in all the time he lived on earth, but when Christians go to heaven they'll be able to look into his wonderful face for ever and ever.'

A deep peace filled the room. Isobel had spoken to Kathryn, and her daughter knew it. And Danny just knew that the day felt good.

All too soon Danny was on the plane back to Wheaton.

On 24th February 1955, mother and daughter said what they knew would be their last goodbyes in their bedroom at home before going to the ship. At the dock, Isobel saw Kathryn's cabin, met those with whom she was to share it, then left with a friend before the ship raised anchor. Everything that was to be said, had been said. It was time for her to go. The friend put her on a train to Wheaton, and, having left Kathryn for the last time, Isobel sped towards her son. What a comfort it was to know that when Kathryn arrived in Singapore her father would be there to meet her.

Over the following months, Isobel Kuhn grew stronger. She and Danny settled down to a pleasant life together, never forgetting their other two family members in far-away places. And the hand that had written a lifetime of letters, turned its attention to writing books. Before long Isobel was speaking at meetings and conferences. Things seemed to be going well with her. But the best was yet to come, and it came while she was attending a Christian camp.

'There's a Mr. George Sutherland on the phone for you,' she was told.

Isobel took the receiver and enjoyed a chat with her friend.

'I've some news for you,' George said, just as Isobel was beginning to wonder why he had called. 'John is on his way home.'

'When?' she gasped.

'Right now.' And she could almost hear George's smile at the end of the phone.

'I'll pick you up when his plane is due in.'

True to his word, as soon as he heard the time of John's arrival, George drove to the camp, collected Isobel and headed for the airport.

Wrapped in the warmth of each other's love, all the years of separation seemed to melt away. John and Isobel

Kuhn luxuriated in the pleasure of their time together, knowing all the while that it would not last long.

'The surgeon says that further surgery would give me a little more time,' she told her husband after a hospital appointment.

'And what do you feel about that?' he asked.

Secure in the knowledge of spending eternity in heaven, neither felt any need to fight for every last possible minute on earth.

'If I still have work to do, I'm prepared to go through with the operation.'

'And have you?' he asked tenderly.

'People tell me I should write more. What do you think?'

'I think you probably should write more, and the surgery would give you time to do that.'

There was an understanding silence between them.

'I can't imagine what it must be like,' Isobel thought aloud, 'to be facing something like this without faith in Jesus.'

John nodded in agreement. 'I don't want to try to imagine it.'

On the last day of 1955, after a happy Christmas with the extended family, Isobel had surgery which was to give her another year of life on earth. But that year was a busy one. Her mornings were spent writing, and afternoons and evenings were taken up with visitors and with times of prayer with John.

'It's a beautiful thing to see you grow ready for

heaven,' a friend told her one day. 'You have such peace.'

There was no pretence in Isobel. 'That's not anything in me,' she said firmly. 'That's all a gift from God. Let me tell you what I do if I take my eyes off Jesus. I think that every headache is a brain tumour, and imagine how I might die of that. And I think of every stomach-ache as cancer of the stomach, and picture the end that would bring. And I've even thought of a twinge of toothache as cancer of the mouth! That's Isobel Kuhn when she takes her eyes off Jesus. Can't you see why I focus so much on him, thanking him over and over again for his presence that gives me peace?'

'Nothing could have made me happier,' Isobel said, easing herself into a comfortable position in her wheelchair. 'Read the letter to me again, John.'

He took the page from her and read. '... so Donald and I are to be married. Think of it! You'll have to write your letters to Mrs. Kathryn Rulison! Dad and Mum, I'm so happy! My only sadness is that you'll not be at our wedding. But we Kuhns have become used to sharing each other's joys long distance.'

'If I'd had to choose a husband for Kathryn, I could have done no better than Donald,' John said. 'He's a fine missionary, and he'll make a fine husband.'

'And because we already know him, we'll be able to picture the wedding and the pair of them setting up home together.'

Early the following year Kathryn and Donald were

married at Chiengmai. Their wedding photos, sent airmail, arrived when Isobel was still able to enjoy them. Weakened by her illness, Isobel could only manage a few words at a time. But she chose them carefully.

'It will soon be time to say goodbye,' she told John, in the middle of March, 1957. He nodded, waiting to see if she would say more, but her energy had gone.

'We've said so many goodbyes over the years,' he said softly, stroking her hand as he spoke. Isobel's lips moved. He bent towards her, willing himself to hear what she was trying to say.

'There will be no more after this one.'

'None,' he agreed. 'There are no partings in heaven.'

Isobel opened her eyes and smiled.

'I'm so looking forward to being there,' she said, 'to being with Jesus for ever.'

A short time later, on 20th March 1957, Isobel and John, who had said goodbye many times over their life together, took their final farewell knowing that they would meet again in heaven, there to be together and with their lovely and loving Lord Jesus for ever and for ever.

Isobel Kuhn - Time line

1901 Isobel Kuhn born
      The United Kingdom launches first
      submarine
1902 Teddy Bear introduced, named after
      American President Theodore Roosevelt
1903 First succesful flight by the Wright brothers
      First silent movies
1904 Construction of the panama canal begins
1905 Albert Einstein develops his theory of
      relativity
1906 San Francisco suffers a violent earthquake
1909 Robert E Peary reaches the North Pole
1912 The Titanic sinks. Largest passenger ship in
      the world at that time.
1914 World War I begins
      Panama Canal completed
1917 America enters the war
      Russian Revolution ends the rule of the
      Tsars
1918 World War I ends
1922 BBC begins transmissions
1923 Mussolini becomes dictator of Italy

1924 France hosts the first Winter Olympics
     Isobel Kuhn is called by God to serve the
     Lisu
1927 Charles Lindbergh. First to fly solo across
     the Atlantic
     Baseball - Babe Ruth hits 60 home runs
1928 Walt Disney makes the first Mickey Mouse
     cartoon
     Isobel Kuhn leaves Canada for China
1929 Alexander Flemming accidentally discovers
     penicillin
1931 The Empire State Building opens in New
     York
1932 Amelia Earhart is the first woman to fly
     solo across the Atlantic
1933 Hitler becomes chancellor of Germany
1939 World War II begins
1941 America enters the war
1945 World War II ends
     First Atomic bombs dropped on Japan
1946 National Health service starts in the U.K.
1950 Petrol and soap rationing ends in the U.K.
1951 Colour T.V. introduced in America
1955 The words 'In God We Trust' appear on all
     American currency
1957 Isobel Kuhn dies

Thinking Further

1 Mrs. Twenty Questions: Christian families

Are those born into Christian families automatically Christians? Does faith in God pass through generations like blue eyes or curly hair?

John 3:1-21   Nicodemus was a religious man, and respectful of Jesus. When he spoke to the Lord, Nicodemus showed he held him in high honour.   Did that make him a believer? What do Jesus' words in 3:3 mean in relation to children from Christian families and 'religious' people?   Isobel Kuhn discovered the truth of Jesus' words that she needed to be born again.

Mark 1:16-17   Does God call us to himself just for our own good, or does he have work for us to do for him?   What were the disciples called to do?   Is it any different for Christians today?

Luke 12:31 In this verse Jesus gives a basic principle on which our lives should be built. What is it? And how does it relate to all our cares and worries and concerns?   (That's outlined in verses 22-31. And it is all summed up in v 34.)

2 In at the Deep End: Falling in love

Isobel Miller and John Kuhn fell in love and were married. We sometimes hear talk of the 'chemistry' of love.   Is that all love is - a chemical reaction?

Genesis 2:18-24   Why did God make the first woman? Remember that everything God made was perfect (Genesis 1:31) so his creation of the first married couple was the creation of something that was perfect. Sadly, Adam and Eve's rebellion (Genesis 3) affected everything, including their marriage and every marriage since. The best of marriages is good, but none are perfect.

God gave the Kuhns a baby, little Kathryn. After reading Psalm 139:13 when does life begin? Is it at conception or not until some months later?

Psalm 139:14-16 Is God interested in the unborn child? What does this have to say to us about abortion and some kinds of genetic engineering?

Proverbs 22:6 What does the Bible say about bringing up children? Should children be left to do what they want? Is disciplining a child a necessity, a responsibility, a duty or an infringement of the child's rights?

3 Greetings and Goodbyes: The Occult

There is a great deal of involvement in the occult today. People read their horoscopes, consult astrologers and engage in many other such things. Deuteronomy 18:10-13 What does God have to say about dabbling in the occult? How does he describe occult ceremonies? In comparison to those who are involved in these evil things, how have God's people to live (v 13)?

Isobel Kuhn's friend had problems because she was married to a non-Christian. 2 Corinthians 6:14-15 What does the Bible say this? What do these verses then say to us about who we should or should not date?

Philippians 1:3-6, Colossians 1:3-8, 1 Thessalonians 1:2-3 When the Kuhns were separated they wrote letters to each other, and so kept the flame of their love burning brightly. Paul loved the churches he founded. Read the beginnings of some of his letters to them.

4 Rainy Season Bible School: Homesickness

When Kathryn Kuhn was just a little girl she was separated from her parents. John and Isobel missed her a lot and no doubt she was often homesick for them. Luke 14:25-27 These verses are very difficult. Does Jesus mean we have to actively hate our families? Or does he mean that we have to love him first, that nothing and nobody should come between us and our Lord? Could that, on rare occasions, even mean that the God-ordained family unit must be parted for a time?

Hebrews 13:5 Does God's Word give comfort in that kind of situation? What is that source of comfort?

James 1:2-6 Can times of trial do us any good? Should we make a positive effort to turn trials into growing experiences? How can we do that?

5 I Have Two Ears Ma-ma: Disability

At the Girls' Bible School it was a blind girl who was the best student. 2 Corinthians 12:7 Is disability a bar to serving God? After all, didn't even the apostle Paul have some sort of health problem?

2 Corinthians 12:9-10 How should the believer cope with health problems and disability? Can such situations even be a benefit in the work of the Lord?

Psalm 27:3-6 The Kuhns were in a war zone, and at times things looked very nasty for them. What do these verses say to those who live in a land that's at war? What's the believer's source of confidence in that situation?

2 Corinthians 7:5-7 There can be wars within us as well as around us. What is our comfort then? What part

do Christians play in supporting each other when they go through tough times? We would be aware of it if our country was at war, and we've all heard of a community spirit that exists in wartime. But are we watchful to see if our friends are going through times of inner conflict, and are we there to support them when they are?

6 In the Firing-line: Ill Health

When Isobel Kuhn was in pain she prayed about it, and she also looked for medical help. Read James 5:13-16 What is our first thought when someone is ill? Is it to call the doctor, or is it to pray? The two go together. After all, any skill a doctor has is a gift from God. But, if we are honest, what is the source of our hope when illness strikes? Is it that the doctor will prescribe something to make us better, or is it the knowledge that God is the Great Physician though he often chooses to work through people he has especially gifted like doctors and nurses?

Galatians 6:2 We all enjoy being with friends who are in good form, when their conversation is amusing, and when the atmosphere is carefree. But do we want to be with them when they are going though bad patches? What does God's Word say about that? Why are we told to help carry each other's burdens?

Galatians 6:10 To whom have we to be especially good?

7 The Long Return to Lisuland: Prayer

Prayer was a very important part of Isobel Kuhn's life. Her prayer times took priority over everything else.

Matthew 14:23 This verse tells us that Jesus, the Son of God, prayed to his Father. What does that say about the Christian's need to pray? Did Jesus pray in a quiet place, or was he able to concentrate on prayer in the middle of a crowd?

Matthew 6:5-15 The Lord Jesus taught his followers to pray. Christians are his modern day followers. What practical guidance does Jesus' teaching give to us? One of the things about prayer that is very difficult to understand, is that God knows what we need before we ask him (v 8), yet he still wants us to ask him. Think of a child with loving parents. They know his needs, but they don't always give him things until he learns to ask for them, e.g. they don't put everything around his place at the table. They wait until he says 'Please may I have...?' before they give him things. Does this throw any light on the subject of prayer?

8 And Danny Makes Four: Teaching

The Kuhns and their colleagues ran Bible Schools in order that young Christians could learn, then go out and teach. They saw their faith as something to be passed on. Mark 5: 19-20 What was Jesus's instruction to the demon-possessed man who was cured and came to faith? What did the man do? And what was the reaction of those who saw and heard him? Do we share our faith, or do we live as though it were a personal interest, only to be engaged in in private?

Romans 10:14-15 Is preaching the only way to spread the Gospel? Can it be chatted about, discussed, shared in informal ways? Think of people with whom you could share your faith. Pray for them before speaking to them.

1 Timothy 4:12 We sometimes think that we are too young to be seriously engaged in reaching out to others with the Gospel. What does Paul's advice to Timothy have to say to us on that subject?

9 'Allo Kafin': Fear

The Kuhns found themselves in some frightening situations. And at some point in our lives we too will have cause to feel fear. Isaiah 43:1 God tells us to 'Fear not' and gives us a reason why we should not fear. What is it? Why does the fact that God has redeemed us release us from fear? Might it be because whatever happens to God's redeemed people here on earth, when they die they will go straight home to heaven and to him?

Isaiah 41:10 In this verse God gives another reason why his people should not be afraid. What is it? This promise is repeated by Jesus in Matthew 28:20.

John 14:6 and Hebrews 13:8 The promise of his presence is only one of many promises made to us by the Lord Jesus. How do these two verses help us to be sure that all these promises will be kept?

Philippians 4:19 In Isobel Kuhn's time of great need, she experienced another of God's promises being kept. Do you think that difficult time threatened her faith or strengthened it?

10 High Drama: Disagreements

Every church has problems. The Lisu church was no

different from the churches we belong to. Acts 15:36-41 This passage describes a 'sharp disagreement' between which two people? Has it ever occurred to you that great men in the early church were mere men, and prone to want their own way just as we do? What does this tell us about putting people on a pedestal? What did Paul and Barnabas do when they disagreed? Did they stay together, niggling away at each other like two terrier dogs and upsetting everyone around them, or did they part company and get on with the work they were doing?

2 Samuel 22:2 Throughout their troubled times, God protects his servants. How did David describe God in his song recorded in this verse? David was hounded for years by King Saul and his henchmen. Find some words that David used to describe God as his protector in Psalm 18. Look especially at the following verses: 1, 2, 14, 30, 32-36 and 39-40.

Ephesians 6:10-18 God arms us against danger. Find the items of armour and think about how we can apply them to ourselves.

11 All Change: Belonging to a family

Despite being separated often, and for long periods of time, family life was very important to the Kuhns. This becomes clear when we read how close they were to each other despite their times apart. Ephesians 6:1-4 gives some ground rules for living peacefully together as a family. Do we find it easier to apply verse 4 rather than verses 1 to 3? But both instructions are equally the Word of God!

Ephesians 5:22-32   How do these verses compare with the modern 'with it' family? Could it be that they are 'without it'? What gives families their stability if it is not the Word of the God who created family life in the beginning? Might it be that disobedience to God's rules is the reason for family breakdowns today?

Ephesians 5:33   Is this verse restricting or fulfilling?

12 Journey's End: Death

Despite surgery, Isobel Kuhn's cancer spread and was the cause of her death. Genesis 3:1-7, 17-19   Illness and death of human beings were not part of God's plan when he created the world. What brought them about?

John 9:1-3   Sickness and death are sometimes the direct result of sin, e.g. drug abuse or immorality. But are they always the direct result of personal sin, or the sins of close family members?

1 Corinthians 15:50-57   What assurance does Paul give regarding the death of believers? Is death the end for them? When they die, has death won a great victory?

Revelation 21:1-4   The Apostle John was given this great vision of heaven, the final home of everyone who trusts in the Lord Jesus Christ. Verse 4 lists some things that will not be found in heaven. What are they? Eternal life means just that, eternal life, life for ever and ever and ever. And what a life!

Dear Reader,

It has been exciting to see how God is continuing to work among the Lisu people and using them to show others the love of Jesus. In China, where it is estimated that over 40% of the 500,000 Lisu are Christians, the government considers the religion of the Lisu to be Christianity! They are the only group of people in China to have this distinction and it brings some privileges to Lisu Christians that other groups don't have. They are free to meet together for worship and there are many Lisu churches in the mountains along the border with Burma. But they are not allowed to have evangelistic meetings. It has only been recently that they have been allowed to open two Short-Term-Bible-Schools for training leaders.

Pray for Lisu Christians to continue to share the good news of Jesus with others. Pray that they will be wise in how they do it.

In Burma about 50% of the 300,000 Lisu are Christians, but they are divided among five different denominations. There have been strong disagreements among the denominations, which has spoiled their witness. Please pray for reconciliation, co-operation and fellowship between Christians of different denominations.

At the moment they are working together to prepare a Lisu Study Bible to help Lisu Christians know God's word better. It has been a joy to see how many of the Lisu Christians have a concern to share the good news of Jesus with other Lisu and to other ethnic groups.

In recent years we have seen over 5,000 Lisu along the China border come to know Jesus through their witness, as well as groups of Hmong and Shan and individuals from other language groups. Pray that they will continue to share the Good News and that God will give them fruit.

Down in Thailand, where there are considerably fewer Lisu (about 25,000), the church has been slower to start. After many years with little progress, the breakthrough came in 1970 when the first three Thailand Lisu families were baptised near Elephant Mountain village.

Since then the church has grown and there are now between 3,000 and 5,000 Christians among the Lisu in Thailand.

Andy and Rose Thomson
Working with the Lisu in Northern Thailand

TRAIL BLAZERS

This is real life made as exciting as fiction! Any Trailblazer title will take you into a world that you have never dreamed of. Have you ever wondered what it would be like to be a hero or heroine? Meet William Wilberforce who fought to bring freedom to millions of slaves. Richard Wurmbrand survived imprisonment and torture. Corrie Ten Boom rescued many Jews from the Nazis by hiding them in a secret room! Amazing people with amazing stories!

A Voice in the Dark: Richard Wurmbrand
Written by Catherine Mackenzie
ISBN 1 85792 2980

The Watchmaker's Daughter: Corrie Ten Boom
Written by Jean Watson
ISBN 1 85792 116X

The Freedom Fighter: William Wilberforce
Written by Derick Bingham
ISBN 1 85792 3715

From Wales to Westminster: Martin Lloyd-Jones
Written by Christopher Catherwood
ISBN 1 85792 3499

The Storyteller: C.S. Lewis
Written by Derick Bingham
ISBN 1 85792 4878

An Adventure Begins: Hudson Taylor
Written by Catherine Mackenzie
ISBN 1 85792 4231

The Children's Champion: George Müller
Written by Irene Howat
ISBN 1 85792 5491

Servant to the Slave: Mary Slessor
Written by Catherine Mackenzie
ISBN 1 85792 3480

PUBLISHING

OMF International works in most East Asian countries, and among East Asian peoples around the world. It was founded by James Hudson Taylor in 1865 as the China Inland Mission. Our overall purpose is to glorify God through the urgent evangelisation of East Asia's billions, and this is reflected in our publishing.

Through our books, booklets, website and quarterly magazine, *East Asia's Billions*, OMF Publishing aims to motivate Christians for world mission, and to equip them for playing a part in it. Publications include:

- contemporary mission issues
- the biblical basis of mission
- the life of faith
- stories and biographies related to God's work in East Asia
- accounts of the growth and development of the Church in Asia
- studies of Asian culture and religion relating to the spiritual needs of her peoples

Visit our website at *www.omf.org*

AUSTRALIA: PO Box 849, Epping, NSW 2121
Freecall 1800 227 154
email: omf-australia@omf.net *www.omf.org*

CANADA: 5759 Coopers Avenue, Mississauga
ON, L4Z 1R9 Toll free 1-888-657-8010
email: omfcanada@omf.ca *www.omf.ca*

HONG KONG: P O Box 70505, Kowloon Central
Post Office, Hong Kong
email: hk@omf.net *www.omf.org*

NEW ZEALAND: P O Box 10-159, Auckland
Tel:09-630 5778
email:omfnz@compuserve.com *www.omf.org*

SINGAPORE: 2 Cluny Road, Singapore 259570
email: sno@omf.net *www.omf.org*

SOUTHERN AFRICA: P O Box 3080, Pinegowrie,
2123 email: za@omf.net *www.omf.org*

UK: Station Approach, Borough Green,
Sevenoaks, Kent, TN15 8BG Tel 01732 887299
email: omf@omf.org.uk *www.omf.org.uk*

USA: 10 West Dry Creek Circle, Littleton, CO
80120-4413 Toll Free 1-800-422-5330   email:
omf@omf.org *www.us.omf.org*

OMF International Headquarters:
2 Cluny Road, Singapore 259570

CHRISTIAN FOCUS

Staying Faithful – Reaching Out!

Christian Focus Publications publishes books for adults and children under its three main imprints: Christian Focus, Mentor and Christian Heritage. Our books reflect that God's word is reliable and Jesus is the way to know him, and live for ever with him.

Our children's publication list includes a Sunday school curriculum that covers pre-school to early teens; puzzle and activity books. We also publish personal and family devotional titles, biographies and inspirational stories that children will love.

If you are looking for quality Bible teaching for children then we have an excellent range of Bible story and age specific theological books.

From pre-school to teenage fiction, we have it covered!

Find us at our web page:
www.christianfocus.com